ALEX COLVILLE

PAINTINGS, PRINTS
AND PROCESSES
1983-1994

ALEX COLVILLE

Edited and written by

Philip Fry

THE MONTREAL MUSEUM
OF FINE ARTS

The exhibition *Alex Colville : Paintings, Prints and Processes, 1983-1994*
was organized by Pierre Théberge, Director, and was shown at the Montreal Museum of Fine Arts
from September 30, 1994, to January 15, 1995.

The exhibition was planned and the catalogue written and edited by Philip Fry, Guest Curator.

The Montreal Museum of Fine Arts
Pierre Théberge, C.Q., *Director*
Mayo Graham, *Chief Curator*
Paul Lavallée, *Director of Administration*
Claude T. Ramsay, *Commercial Director*
Danielle Sauvage, *Director of Communications*

This catalogue is a production of the Publications Service of the Montreal Museum of Fine Arts.

Co-ordination:
Denise L. Bissonnette

Revision:
Donald Pistolesi

Graphic Design:
Primeau Dupras

Photo-engraving and stripping:
Grafix Studio

Printing:
Metropole Litho Inc.

Photographs were taken by:

The Douglas Udell Gallery, Edmonton, p. 157, 159, 161

The Drabinsky Gallery, Toronto, p. 81, 99, 145, 147, 153, 165, 167, 169

The Montreal Museum of Fine Arts: Bernard Brien, Brian Merrett
Photos of the artist: Christine Guest

Ned Pratt, p. 149

Royal Bank of Canada, p. 35

Thomas Moore Photography, Toronto, p. 63, 65

Richard-Max Tremblay, p. 87
as well as the owners of the works

ISBN: 2-89192-186-0

Legal deposit - 4th trimester 1994
Bibliothèque nationale du Québec
National Library of Canada

PRINTED IN CANADA

THE MONTREAL MUSEUM OF FINE ARTS
P.O. Box 3000, Station "H"
Montreal, Québec H3G 2T9

Contents

TIME AS THE CROW FLIES
*Viewing Alex Colville's
Recent Work*

Acknowledgements

Before meeting Alex Colville to discuss the feasibility of this exhibition, I read Helen Dow's *The Art of Alex Colville* and David Burnett's *Colville*. Although I have not quoted these books directly in the text, they form a background to my interest in the drawings and to what I have written. I am also grateful to David Burnett for his aid with various practical aspects of this show. Marilyn Schiff Burnett has been of particular help to me, providing documents, tracking down works and permitting me to use the numbering of her catalogue raisonné in this publication.

My research assistant was Leslie Mitchell. She was directly involved in the selection and documentation of the drawings included in the exhibition and contributed to the geometric analyses of the paintings and prints. I am grateful for her understanding and patience midst an overwhelming mass of documents.

The personnel of the Montreal Museum of Fine Arts has worked on this exhibition with exemplary competence and enthusiasm. I am indeed grateful for this. However, because Donald Pistolesi, who edited the English text, and Jean-Paul Partensky, who prepared the French translation, have been so intimately involved over a long period with what I have attempted to say, I would like to express my particular appreciation for their strong sense of positive collaboration and their respectful, painstaking labour.

Alex Colville has made my work as curator of the exhibition a source of discovery, joy and satisfaction. He has offered his insights willingly, he has responded generously to my questions and doubts, and in particular, he has encouraged me to be free in my attempt to see and interpret his work directly, with a personal view. For all this, and especially his trust, I thank him deeply. And to Rhoda Colville I would like to say a special thanks, for opening her home to me and to my collaborators, for the chowder at lunch, for her gentle wisdom, for her friendship.

Philip Fry

The Old Field Garden and
the University of Ottawa

One of Canada's most important twentieth-century artists, Alex Colville creates paintings which guide us to look at the world with fresh eyes.

Alex Colville was immediately responsive to our proposal to prepare an exhibition of his oeuvre from this last decade for the Montreal Museum of Fine Arts. We are honoured by his collaboration and very grateful to him for his enthusiasm, unflagging interest and support.

Similarly, Philip Fry, the Guest Curator of the exhibition, has been an exceptional friend and professional. While continuing his teaching in the Visual Arts Department of the University of Ottawa, he devoted himself to the task, albeit pleasurable, of exploring and describing Colville's world. We are led by the magic of his words through the pictorial space of the paintings and prints.

The exhibition and this catalogue present nearly four hundred works by Alex Colville. The fact that the majority of these are preparatory drawings that have never before been shown provides some indication of the tremendous organization involved in preparing the exhibition. I extend my thanks to all the employees of the Museum who participated in this project. Particular mention should be made of Mayo Graham, Chief Curator, Pierre Archambault, her Administrative Assistant, Johanne Perron, Works on Paper Conservator and Denise L. Bissonnette, Head of the Publications Service.

Of course, such an outstanding exhibition is only possible with the co-operation of the lenders, who have agreed to part with their works. We are indebted to these private collectors, galleries, museums and corporations.

We are grateful for the ongoing support of the Quebec Ministère de la Culture et des Communications to the Museum's operations. We also extend our very grateful appreciation to the Conseil des arts de la Communauté urbaine de Montréal.

It is hoped that this exhibition, which provides a rich landscape of the most recent years of Alex Colville's creativity, will be a resource and inspiration for our Museum audience.

Pierre Théberge, C.Q.
Director of the Montreal Museum of Fine Arts

Preface

TIME AS THE CROW FLIES

*Viewing
Alex Colville's
Recent Work*

Entrance

Two paintings by Alex Colville in the collection of the Montreal Museum of Fine Arts, the one entitled *Cyclist and Crow,* the other, *Church and Horse,* hang with accompanying drawings in the entrance to this exhibition. Painted in 1981 and 1964 respectively, they predate the period of Colville's work featured here, 1983 to 1994. Their presence is intended to remind us of the artist's past accomplishments and the quality of his contribution to our cultural life, and to provide an opportunity to review some of the main features of his production preliminary to viewing the recent work.

It is a tranquil moment of summer. In the foreground of the picture, to the left, separating us from a shimmering field of barley, a cyclist turns her head in the direction of a crow winging its way to the right, skimming low over the ripening crop. Midmorning light pours into the scene from the upper left; flowing gently over the field in waves of blue-green, rosy browns, chartreuse and tender leaf hues, the light is caught up, refracting and flashing in the wiry bristles of the barley, transforming them into translucent white wings lifting opaque, cylindrical bodies of seed towards the invisible sky. In places the light seems to condense – as a sheen, for example, on the leading edge of the crow's visible wing or as a highlight on the curved contour of the cyclist's back. Gently the light caresses and warms the woman's bare arms and legs, describing their full, rounded shapes, though it glares coldly in its sharp delineation of the bicycle's metallic frame. Strangely, although shading has been used to model volumes, to suggest masses and textures, Alex Colville's *Cyclist and Crow* contains no cast shadows.

As we allow ourselves to become absorbed in this luminous rural scene, what we first saw and admired as an accurate depiction, a true-to-life view of the undulating sweep of the field and the parallel movement of the cyclist and crow, gives way to an obscure feeling that something about the picture escapes our immediate grasp, that something elusive, something fugitive is happening here which inspires a sentiment akin to awe. In the cyclist's ride, in the bird's flight, in the limpid flow of light which strangely suffuses the scene, there is an uncanny stillness. The rider speeds along, but neither she nor her bicycle moves; the crow surges forward on a strong downbeat of its powerful wings, but floats static, forever fixed in place over the waves of barley. The cyclist's left leg is just beginning to push down on the pedal on which her foot is positioned horizontally, and her right leg has lifted just slightly so that only her toes rest on the metal cleats, graphically portraying the circular gesture which should propel the bicycle forward. But their movement suspended, these legs communicate no impulsion to the bicycle which nevertheless stands on its spokeless wheels as if in motion. The cyclist is not entering the picture from somewhere else, nor will she ever get to its other side; she is simply present, here in this scene, her head forever turned to the side, like this. The crow's wings never did beat downward, forcing a rush of summer air through their splayed flight feathers, and never will rise in the complementary action of flight; the dark bird of wisdom and ruse, fateful omen, hovers forever perfectly still, casting no shadow, making no advance in the excessive clarity of this summer morning.

The world on view in *Cyclist and Crow* involves no time whatsoever, neither as a transformation of things forging ahead from past to future, nor as the duration of a state of affairs which holds its own against the onslaught of change. What we viewers of this work are given is the *shape* of a fugitive instant, a peculiar, momentary coincidence

A. CYCLIST AND CROW, 1981

Acrylic polymer emulsion on Masonite,
70.6 x 100 cm
The Montreal Museum of Fine Arts, gift of Lavalin, Inc.

of things presented as a timeless, self-contained world. Here, the flow of time has been reduced to a quintessential, indivisible point of awareness, an eternal present which is projected or laid out in spatial terms as a construction of visible relationships, as an image. The disquieting effect of this work seems to be triggered as we notice, however vaguely, that standing in its still, endless present, the picture invokes our consciousness as viewers immersed, inextricably projected onward, in time. It illuminates and heightens our sensitivity to the fleeting and mysterious experience which we call *being present.*

Our sense of time seems to arise within us when we experience change as part of our human condition; we see outward, always outward, not only from the spatial centre of our self but from a personal *now* which, mercurial as midnight, flows on inexorably, escaping our grasp in the very instant of its realization. The tragedy of our condition is that we are thus condemned: never to stand still, never to dwell within our self; ever to be cast outward from within, holding close to the things we experience only through their representation as mental images. Nothing happens twice. What remains with us, in us, of the present is a memory of our awareness, a sense of being, and *images* that live as phantoms in our hearts and minds, shifting, changing, transforming their shapes as they attempt to embody the particular sentiment we have of our self – our self-image, our identity. From outside our personal life-worlds, *Cyclist and Crow,* an image forever the same, invites us to *notice* the mystery of the present moment, the place from which time flies straight onward as the crow, laden with choice and fate.

If we pause to reflect on our experience of *Cyclist and Crow,* one of the things we might want to ask ourselves is how Colville has used the art of painting to involve us so deeply in the scene. With few exceptions – notably the "movement" paintings of Marcel Duchamp (from *Dulcinée* to the *Passage of the Virgin to the Bride*), and the key works of the Futurists (such as Giacomo Balla's *Dynamism of a Dog on a Leash*) – paintings in the Occidental tradition normally exclude time deliberately, offering us instead a simultaneous presentation of forms as constituents of a purely visual or pictorial space. Even Braque's and Picasso's radical investigations of what knowledge has to do with how we perceive things retain simultaneity as an essential principle of figurative construction; in Cubist works, various aspects or facets of the subject are assembled, not in a temporal sequence, but as complementary, constitutive views existing in a synchronic present. We are, in fact, so used to the convention of simultaneity in paintings that we rarely even notice that they abolish time. We feel the dynamic tensions of forms; we talk about "what is going on" in an image and blithely place parentheses around the fact that nothing is actually happening there at all. Why, then, do we feel the absence of time so acutely in *Cyclist and Crow*?

Part of the answer no doubt lies in Colville's choice to represent the figures of the woman and the crow at critical instants in the cycle of their respective gestures. This depiction *implies* time by requiring us, in the name of plausibility, to supply a past and to project a future for what appears to be an arrested moment within a programme of movement. But focussing on each figure's ability to suggest movement – something which is found in many other artists' work – though important as a point of departure in our investigation, does not help us come to terms with the peculiar experience of time we feel as essential in *Cyclist and Crow*. A fuller answer seems to lie in Colville's use of his medium, his individual application of the conventions of painting, in order to construct a total, coherent pictorial situation concerned with temporal relationships.

A comparison with photography might help to centre our attention on the effects which arise from an artist's choice and use of a given medium. Although Colville's depiction of gesture seems similar to the "captured" or "frozen" movement of still photography, the comparison seems limited to the fact that both types of imagery require that we understand something about the relationships between the parts that make up the subject's static configuration – the function of feet on pedals, for example, or the flapping of wings – as a prerequisite to the recognition of implicit movement. In practice, though, we do not seem to deal with the painted portrayal and the photographic representation of gesture in the same way. For instance, many of us spontaneously see and interpret "stop-action" photographs as recordings of past events, as instants *taken* from the flow of history, as discrete, individualized moments which forever recede from us into an ever more distant past. It is also interesting to note that in photography there is a kind of concordance between the technology of visual recording and the movement of the subject: to "freeze" a swiftly moving subject, a "rapid" exposure and a "fast" film are used. The product of this concordance between "high-speed" photography and a moving subject, indeed its very purpose, is, as suggested by Marcel Duchamp's reflections on his ultrarapid *Bride,* to present the subject in a state of instantaneous rest. This state exists, never in itself, but only as a technologically determined relationship. In short, our impression that the "stop-action" image affords us a "truth" about the subject depends to a large extent on our assumptions about photography as a medium of representation.

In striking contrast to the photographic image, what happens in *Cyclist and Crow* appears as the embodiment of a mental image through the exercise of the painter's competence as an artist, what could be called a "slow" and "body-centred" technology. The painted gesture is a construct of the imagination; it has not been *taken* or *abstracted* from time, but *made* to open before us in an absolute present, soliciting not observation, but personal participation. It is re-created or updated each time it is contemplated.

When we look at a painting, we are doing much more than receiving a visually encoded message or grasping what we suppose to be the artist's intention. We are at work. We *produce,* through the interplay of our feelings and knowledge, the bearing or import of the picture, its content; we *complete* the work of the artist by applying what we have learned from our own lives, by putting ourselves and our assumptions about painting on the line as we interpret what we have been given to see. In our attempt to clarify the bearing of *Cyclist and Crow* it might therefore be useful for us to recall some of the general characteristics of painting with the purpose of highlighting the specific means used by Colville.

The expression "pictorial space" refers to the image world we discover within the frame of a picture – the total effect of extension and depth, light and colour, volumes, masses and textures which displays itself to us as we become involved in a picture. No matter how spontaneously it seems to appear before our eyes, pictorial space depends for its existence on an activity of our perception and our minds – we *choose* to look at the colours and lines the artist has placed on a surface not for what they are literally, painted brush strokes, but metaphorically, that is, *as if* they were the constitutive elements of a space. Contours, shading and texture provide an impression of volume because these are clues by which we individualize objects in our daily lives, but we know that no solid object stands there in the picture; overlapping, diminution of relative size, shifts in colour or value and the reduction of detail indicate depth, but we know there is no space inside the surface, behind the picture plane. As we stop looking *at* the surface and see *into* the picture, we create a discontinuity between the space of the everyday world and the imaginary space marked off from the wall by the work's frame. Distinct from the everyday world and self-contained, pictorial space is not an autonomous reality. It exists as a *relationship* between a painted surface and our minds. We *generate* it, using what we see in the picture as a key to the whole bank of images and thoughts through which we have set in memory, sorted out and given direction to our life experiences. Because we know that we are dealing with *signs* of things rather than the things themselves, we can decide what degree of plausibility we want to apply as we investigate a pictorial space – we easily recognize that some pictures "stretch" our imagination more than others. Some tax our abilities so much that we find it difficult to "get into" them. What seems most important to note in this connection is that, while metaphorical seeing is based on our day-to-day experiences, it is always mediated by the imagination and therefore never directly reproduces scenes or happenings of the everyday world. A painting, even should it attempt to describe an event objectively, is primarily and ultimately a construction of the artist's mind, of his or her ability to conceive a mental image, to give it form and to externalize it in a material shape that can be shared.

The key which allows us to enter a pictorial space is the vantage point adopted by the artist during the work's construction. It is from this viewpoint that the artist envisions how the pictorial space will be laid out, how the various elements of the image will be distributed and from what angle they will be seen. When using the conventions of one- or two-point perspective, for example, if an object is presented from the front we will never see its back. Some artists accept this kind of limitation because of the expressive power perspective gives them. Others have worked out different rules to find their way around the constraints of traditional systems of perspective. In practice, vantage points used to construct the pictorial space of a painting are highly specific, varying widely according to the artist's style and the requirements of the image being produced. Analytic Cubism, in its attempt to account for the way we build up our understanding of objects by assembling the various things we can see and know about them, proposes its subject matter from several viewpoints at the same time; in the same vein, Synthetic Cubism constructs its pictures while taking into account how its subject matter could or would be perceived from various points of view. Many forms of nonobjective painting, especially those related to Jackson Pollock's "all-over" approach, attempt to root themselves in the everyday world according to the physical, literal conditions of their medium and reject fixed viewpoints altogether, adopting instead moving positions that scan rather than look into the picture's surface. This creates an optical space of fluctuating depth explicitly anchored to the picture plane. If in dealing with an individual image, the artist chooses a very high viewpoint, the pictorial space tends to be flattened out, and there is an insinuation of domination or control over the subject matter. The choice of a low viewpoint can open up the space, but it tends to imply submission to the subject matter. In putting a chosen vantage point to use, the artist also becomes involved in decisions about how the surface is to be treated as a flat pattern, a system of positions and distances up, down and sideways that has its own structure at the same time it indicates relationships between things located within the pictorial space.

When an artist decides that a painting is finished, he or she abandons the physical position in front of the work that located and specified the vantage point during execution. Left vacant and open, this position – along with its conventions – is the one we adopt as we view the work.

In *Cyclist and Crow* the viewpoint is most easily determined by taking into account what we can see of the bicycle's handlebars. We look down upon them just slightly from somewhat to their right, which locates us a bit forward of the woman, our eyes level with her head and the bird in flight. The important thing here is that we are not situated as observers, sitting on a verandah, for example, or even standing at the other side of the road watching the cyclist speed past. We are riding along parallel to the cyclist, we are her companions, we share her view. Whether we attempt to think of ourselves as on a bicycle or, perhaps, as monitoring the ride from a car does not seem to matter as much as the sense of participation generated by adopting the artist's viewpoint: we belong in this scene just as the woman does. Her glance guides ours, her involvement in a moment of awareness models our perception and recognition of the

A.03

passing instant. Our viewpoint is subjective, involving us in the event. Unlike experiences of everyday life, where nothing really ever happens more than once, as often as we enter an image from the proposed viewpoint, the same key relationships recur in a stable configuration. Imaginary because it exists only as a pictorial reality, and abstract because it holds itself outside the inexorable flow of time, this configuration works in the manner of a mental flashlight, assisting us as we seek to illuminate – to reveal to ourselves – what lies within those special moments of experience to which we hold strongly in memory and which we treasure as central to our personal history.

Cyclist and Crow conveys a peculiar feeling of perfect factual determination: what until this moment could have been a question of chance has become absolute in the coincidence of a glance and the flight of a bird. One of the main pictorial factors that contributes to this feeling is the way the surface of the painting has been organized through the placement and shapes of the various figures and through the relationships established between them. When we are directly involved in what is being shown in a painting, we do not necessarily notice the play of proportions, the balance of tensions, the vectors of implicit movement that arise from the distribution of shapes over its surface. We even forget that the surface itself is presented within the arbitrary limits of its framing edges. We intuit these things, we grasp them directly as part of the whole image, we feel their effect. It is when we ask ourselves why and how the image makes us feel a certain way that we start to observe the mechanisms put to work in its construction. Some of these are fairly obvious, others will appear if we play with the image in an attempt to discover its secrets, and yet others will perhaps lie hidden during our investigations, awaiting, to reveal themselves, some clue from the artist or those more versed in the intricacies of geometry and mathematics. The geometric sketches which illustrate this essay were prepared by the artist on request.

Several systems for regulating the distribution of surface features are used with sufficient frequency in Colville's work to warrant a pause here. One, a ratio producing the "golden section" or "golden mean", has been used since Greek antiquity and is relatively familiar; the other three, though also rooted in mathematics, are less well known as regulating tools in art.

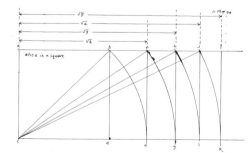

The "golden ratio" can be used to determine the unequal division of a line known as its "golden section" or to set up a harmonious proportion between the width and the height of a "golden rectangle". The golden section falls on a line AB at point C in such a way that the shorter segment CB is to the longer segment AC as the longer segment AC is to the whole line AB. A golden rectangle is formed when the proportion of the shorter side of a rectangle is to the longer side as the longer side is to the combined length of the shorter and longer sides. In mathematical terms, the proportion of the segmented line or the sides of the rectangle thus obtained works out to approximately 1 : 1.618, or roughly 3 to 5.

To establish the overall proportions or format of a work, Colville also uses a geometric system which produces an internally related series of rectangles. The generation of the rectangles begins with a square. The top and the bottom of the square are extended outward to the right, their length for the moment left indeterminate. The lower left-hand corner of the square is then used as a position to place the pivoting point of a compass. The compass is extended to the upper right-hand corner of the square, that is, the length of the square's diagonal, and an arc is dropped until it cuts the lower external extension of the square. From this point, a vertical line is drawn to meet the upper external extension of the square, forming a closed figure known as a "root-2" rectangle. If, using the same lower left-hand corner and the upper right corner of the new root-2 rectangle, another arc is dropped to the lower extension of the square, and a vertical is drawn to close the form, a root-3 rectangle is produced. If the upper right-hand corner of the root-3 rectangle is used in the same way, a root-4 rectangle is produced, and so on up to root-8 and root-9. What is important to bear in mind is that while each rectangle has its own characteristics and affinities with other geometric forms, each successive rectangle in the series contains the structure of its predecessors, and they are moreover all related by their common system of generation. This gives rise to a set of geometric proportions or rhythms as well as to a sense of internal necessity. The judicious placement of figures using the main structural divisions of these rectangles can then serve to establish locations and intervals on the painted surface that partake of the absolute order of geometry.

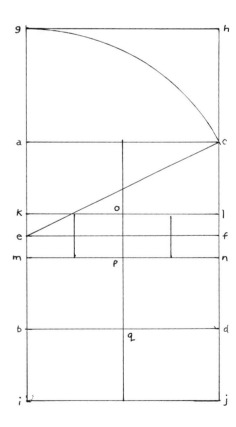

Colville uses a geometric construction known as Le Corbusier's "Modulor" with some frequency. Originally devised for architecture, Le Corbusier's system is generated by placing a square ABDC within two contiguous squares, GKLH and KIJL forming GIJH, in such a way that the horizontal median of ABDC, EF, meets JH at the position F, which is called "the place of the right angle". The right angle is formed by inscribing lines from the corner I to F and from F to the corner G. Once the median of square ABDC is placed according to the place of the right angle, a series of equivalences and proportional differences appear, producing a set of harmonious modular units with strong affinities to the golden ratio and the root-2 and root-5 rectangle. Since the rectangular units produced in this manner are modular, the originating figure can be partially truncated or extended without losing its regulatory capacity as long as the proportional system is respected. Note that there is a slight discrepancy in the system, which shows up near the corner G.

A mathematical sequence named the "Fibonacci series" also appears in Colville's work as a regulatory system. The series is produced by adding each new number to the preceding number, thereby creating increasingly larger but proportional intervals: 1, 1, 2, 3, 5, 8, 13, 21, 34, 55, etc. Once the proportion of 2 to 3 appears in the sequence, the ratios between successive pairs tend to gravitate around the golden proportion.

A.01

Whatever the system used to regulate the surface of a work, it does not, in itself, guarantee success or failure. It is a predisposition, a set of related possibilities available for use. Everything depends on the way these possibilities are exploited by the artist to embody or construct an image world.

One way of approaching the surface organization of *Cyclist and Crow* is to ask what factors in its construction contribute to the impression of movement from left to right and how these focus on the glance between the woman and the bird. The format of the painting is that of a horizontal rectangle approximately seven-tenths the height of its width, which suggests the use of a root-2 rectangle. The effect of lateral spread and implicit side-to-side movement established by this format is accentuated by actual and virtual horizontal divisions of the surface. Near the top of the image, a railway line separates the field of barley from the narrow band of dense bush which runs parallel to the top of the painting. This arrangement is echoed, in softer delineation, by the bare soil which borders the picture's lower edge. The bicycle's wheels, occupying exactly one-half the height of the image, mark the surface's virtual partition into equal upper and lower areas; these in turn feature horizontal divisions separated by proportioned gaps or rhythmic intervals. If, for example, the vertical edges of the picture are marked at their upper golden sections and these points are joined, the resulting virtual line running at the level of the bicycle seat and the cyclist's hand follows the indistinct edge where the erect barley stalks end their rise and their heads recede into the distance to form the flowing surface of the field. With the gently rolling undulations of the crop, the lateral spread of the image becomes a horizontal flow, and directionality is established not only from what we know about the leading edges of moving bicycles and flying crows, but also by the virtual sight line, parallel to the railway tracks and situated at our viewing level, which passes with a turn of our head from the woman's invisible eyes to the bird.

Another striking thing about this painting is that, although the image is most densely massed in its left sector, what could create a sense of imbalance is turned into a tension, an implicit movement to the right, by the structure of the space as well as the shape and placement of the figures. If we take our cue from the poles along the railway track to divide the picture vertically, we may observe that the resulting divisions are situated one-seventh of their width to the right of a symmetrical, balanced partition. To the left side of the picture, only one-seventh of the space between the poles is shown and, at the right side, one-seventh of the space is absent. The divisions fall such that the beak of the crow just barely passes the line which separates the arrangement of figures in "movement" from the "vacant" area to the right, and the next cut to the left passes through the sprocket of the bicycle's front wheel, repeating the way the left framing edge shears off half of the back wheel. Between these two divisions, the crow's tail lines up with the forward edge of the front wheel.

The shapes of the figures heighten their implicit action. The curved back of the cyclist, repeating the arc of the bicycle's front fender, weighs down and forward on her arms, mirroring the upward thrust of the machine's frame. If this triangulation of forms produces a vectorial forward thrust, it also includes the flight of the dartlike bird as part of its dynamics: the lines of vision initiated by the bars of the bicycle's frame pass virtually into the space forward and above, crossing like scissors and latching onto the bird in a deft pincer movement. The woman's head turns towards the bird in flight. In the instant that we are given to see as participants, a tenuous connection takes place. A fleeting glance happens. It is not just a possibility. It is determined, necessary, absolute. It is forever.

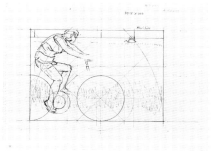

A.02

Among Colville's preparatory drawings for *Cyclist and Crow*, two, dated 3 and 4 July 1981, show the geometry which governs the layout of the picture and, while confirming some of our observations, clarify how the whole image holds together as one pattern. The format of the picture is a root-2 rectangle whose generating square is located within the rectangle twice: one time so that its left side corresponds with the left side of the picture; the other so that its right corresponds to the picture's right-hand border. The bicycle and woman fit perfectly into the left square, the front tire occupying its whole lower right-hand quadrant and the woman's body curving through the upper left quadrant so that her head just touches the square's perpendicular centre line. In this arrangement, the space outside the square contains only the distance to be traversed by the cyclist and, high above, by the crow. With the right-hand inscription of the square, a regulating arc and a perpendicular line intersect at the point which corresponds to the position of the pole along the railway tracks behind the woman's head, establishing the slightly off-centre displacement to the right that we noticed above. A more detailed examination of the drawings reveals further elaborations of the pattern – as, for example, in the inscription of circles and the use of the railway line as the top of yet another square – and demonstrates conclusively that the artist is dealing here not only with the placement of isolated figures but with a coherent system of intervals, a rhythmic structure based on the distances between things.

Looking now not *at* the surface of the picture but *into* its depth, the salient fact would seem to be that the action portrayed is located up front, in the area defined by the foreground and middle ground. The cyclist and her machine are so close to the picture plane that the bottoms of the bicycle's tires run along the work's framing edge and the barley rises as an opaque vertical plane not far behind, emphasizing the shallowness of the foreground. The middle ground is defined by the diminution and colour changes of the barley heads as they recede towards the back of the field; although the crow's exact position is difficult to determine – our main cue is its relative size – it apparently flies much closer to the front of the field than to the back. The background, rising as a wall of bush and trees behind the railway tracks, is really more like a backdrop cutting off vision than a space opening into the far distance.

The principles of linear perspective as applied in *Cyclist and Crow* (once again the handlebars can be used as a cue, but we can also note as an indication of the construction that the woman's left arm is not completely overlapped by her right arm and that we see her legs from somewhat in front and above) seem to be used mainly to set up and highlight what is going on between the main figures or "actors" in the picture. If Classical representation constructed a deep pictorial space which receded towards one or more vanishing points in the far distance, Neoclassical painting tended to interrupt this spatial recession by blocking the view between the middle ground and the background with a wall or some other opaque plane while placing figures towards the front in a side-to-side distribution. There are quite plausible reasons for this change in approach beyond those having to do with purely visual effects. The Classical construction still serves to reveal to us what was understood when it was being developed as the divinely appointed, intrinsic order of things, whereas the Neoclassical emphasizes human action on the stage of life. Similar to the Neoclassical construction in that it features implicit lateral movement situated to the front of the picture, *Cyclist and Crow* differs in the implications of its dynamics. The glance embodied in this picture draws us beyond the world of human affairs into the mysterious zone of our relationship with nature.

Colville's treatment of the figurative aspects of *Cyclist and Crow* exemplifies the same exactitude as the work's geometrical plan, carefully balancing the need to retain the picture's visual unity while differentiating and identifying the components of its subject matter. No doubt central to the aura of determined necessity, of the absolute, the picture's unity is assured by the overall tone or colour range as well as by the various figures' inscription in the regulatory pattern. The brilliance of that summer morning suffuses the whole picture, holding everything together in what we sense to be a family of colours. But the setting, although it informs our understanding and contributes positively to the dynamics of the image, is not to be confused with the figures in which the implicit action is focussed. The necessary differentiation is achieved mainly through the use of clearly defined dividing or contour lines, the use of local or descriptive colour, and the representation of appropriate textural characteristics. Common to the approach of many – though not all – painters, in Colville's hands the use of these techniques produces figures that stand somewhere between an ideogram or pictogram and the visual description of a particular person or thing.

If we compare the continuous line which defines the contours of the cyclist to the broken delimitation of figures which characterizes Cézanne's mature work, what becomes immediately apparent is a major difference in the way the figures affirm their presence. In Cézanne's approach, breaks in contour lines create visual passages between the inside and the outside of figures; the viewer's eye, moving through the gaps, knits the figures and the surrounding space together into a homogeneous unit.

The figure loses not only much of its volume as it ebbs and flows with the surrounding space, but its ability to express individuality and independence as well, sacrificing these dimensions of existence to a pictorial pattern in which each part is treated as subservient to the whole, as an intersection in a field of energies. The sentiment of presence arises in this context more from the dynamics of the pictorial space as a system than from the perception of a specific site or source, a body, to which the viewer can impute subjective activity within the picture. Colville's cyclist is detached from her surroundings by a sharp, continuous contour which delineates her shape and contains her volume. Although related to the space around her, indeed to the space of the whole picture, through her conformity to its underlying geometric regulatory pattern, she is perceived as a self-contained, distinct and autonomous figure. Alone within the confines of her body, she acts, she is aware, she is present. But who is she to us, this faceless woman glancing at a crow?

Deprived forever of a view of the woman's face, there is much that we will never know. We cannot, at least with certitude, give her a name, for it is on faces that personal identity is most clearly written. We cannot see in her gaze, in the expression of her mouth, how she feels at this moment, whether she is surprised, challenged or perhaps awed by the flight of the bird. We do see, in the attitude of her body, that she is attentive to what is happening. But as we seek to deepen our knowledge of her, we find other absences that thwart our search. The perfectly modelled and textured volumes of her arms and legs and the clothing she wears display a minimum of descriptive detail. Straining muscles and taut tendons do not swell and ripple in their characteristically individual ways under her skin, and no scars or blemishes speak of her history or mark her identity. No details of tailoring, no dirt or sweat stains, no signs of wear appear on her otherwise ordinary sleeveless sweater and shorts; no scuff marks mar the spanking new appearance of her running shoes. Her face hidden, we cannot share the woman's interior state, the unfolding of her feelings, her psychology, and without descriptive details for cues, we cannot share in her personal history. We know more about her than what we would find in a conceptual diagram of woman-in-general, but less than in a minute description of an individual.

Why would Colville have presented the woman cyclist this way? It seems to me that her peculiar status as an image – neither general nor particular, neither totally conceptual nor completely concrete, but somewhere in between – allows her to act as a site for the display of a pure pattern of awareness. Because nothing calls attention to the woman's individuality, she cannot be distant like a stranger; with nothing standing in the way, we can focus on her momentary tie with the bird and identify ourselves as participants, her virtual companions. Unashamedly, since personal invasion is not an issue, we model our glance on hers. The instant of awareness becomes ours; we share in an abstract moment of instantaneous rest.

Marked by a similar absence of particularizing detail, eveything else in the picture participates in the cyclist's in-between status. Though painted with painstaking accuracy – there exist preparatory drawings in which Colville noted the precise dimensions of the bicycle parts and the manner of their assemblage – the image shows the Peugeot bicycle as if it were brand-new, without dints or rust, without mud and dust, without a history. It functions in the image less as an object individualized by use than as one instance in a series of production, a model. Its importance as an object resides primarily in the fact that it gives a shape and implicit movement to the cyclist's means of displacement.

The field of barley has likewise been envisioned as growing outside the vicissitudes of time and place. To the front, each plant seems to rise on its stem, some sporting a bent leaf, until it terminates in light-refracting bristles, forming with its neighbours a low wall of blue-green. Along the roadside grow no obstructive grasses or wildflowers, in amongst the barley no bindweed tangles around the stalks, no thistles prepare to launch their down. If the spacing close-up does not make the barley heads seem numerous enough to account for the massed stems, with recession into the distance the pattern, becoming much denser, suggests a sea of glistening waves, and we feel this to be an image of plenty, of unencumbered bounty. The crop, fruit of the farmer's collaboration with nature, will be copious and clean. Over the field flies a solitary bird. It is not just any bird, but a crow.

Like the cyclist and the bicycle, this crow is presented neither as an individual among others of its kind nor as a pure concept of a species. It flies there, wings forever outstretched over the field, an exemplary image. A scavenger and a survivor, smaller relative of the raven, the crow is a sly opportunist, a calculator, a thief. As this bird lives on the misfortune of others, its presence is ominous, laden with foreboding. It cries havoc and announces catastrophe. But it is also wise, prudent and circumspect, occupying an important niche in the regenerative cycle of nature. By feeding on death, it gives life. It typifies the duality of nature, the threatening, violently destructive powers that erupt during the shaping of events as well as the generous flow of life-giving, nurturing and ecstatic creative energies that make our world happen to be.

In the instant we share with the cyclist, in that glance we cast with her towards the crow, a model is proposed, a standard set up against which we can measure ourselves. Aware, we gauge our speed, our use of time, by the flight of the crow – faster, slower, synchronized perhaps. The darkling bird wings straight forward, casting no shadow upon the crop so full of promise. It would seem that we are not being invited so much to judge what has been done as to consider possibilities for the future, the choices to be made as we cover ground. Can we learn to recognize, accept and work with the ambiguity of natural forces and, in doing so, live out our time as the crow flies?

Attentive, we measure ourselves against the bird. But how does it, awesome creature destined to fly the border between death and life, how does *it* measure *itself*?

In *Church and Horse,* you are just at the point of entering an untended churchyard blanketed in a low growth of yellow-green and brown vegetation. You are not very tall, not tall enough even to see over the top rail of the fence. You hesitate for a moment before the gateway, a bit to the right of its centre. The white metal-tubing-and-wire gate is askew. The left gatepost, in disrepair, has risen somewhat above the level of its companion and lists noticeably towards the left. Facing you monumentally, with a closed door directly in your line of sight, looms a white clapboard church, returning your gaze with its blank, windowless stare. The flat, symmetrical façade blocks your view; only the bits of receding roofline indicate the interior volume of the building. To the back of the bleak structure, on both sides, the yard seems to disappear down a slope. From behind the top of the decline, to your right, rises the slate grey prismatic mass of a tombstone. As you read the sign that, set above the doorway, identifies the church and welcomes everyone, from the right a darksome horse thunders in silence across the yard, its hooves soundlessly flailing the air, never touching the ground. Though the animal casts no shadow, bluish highlights on its head and body, perhaps the glistening of sweat, reflect the cool, diffused light shed by a pewter-toned sky. Its features self-absorbed, its demeanour implacable, the horse gallops precipitously towards the open gate you are about to enter.

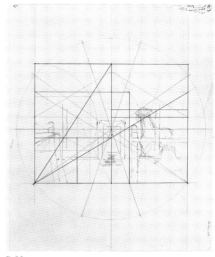

B.03

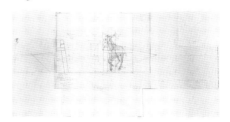

B.06

The format of this picture is based on two equal golden rectangles set vertically side by side; the virtual line created where they abut runs through the peak of the church's roof and the centre of the sign, door and steps, but somewhat to the right of the open gateway's centre. If the image is divided into golden sections from both top and bottom, the upper of the two resulting horizontals runs through the same portion of the capitals on both sides of the church, but the lower one runs along the bottom edge of the fence rail on the left and the top edge of the rail to the right. The horizontal produced by projecting the rooflines of the church downward to the sides of the picture and joining the points thus established brushes by the sphere at the top of the left gatepost and runs across the top of the door's decorative lintel but, too high to meet the top of the right gatepost, touches instead upon the horse's flaring nostril. The surface pattern of the picture exploits the format in two ways: the centred and horizontally symmetrical co-ordinates bind the church tightly to the format's main axes, producing an effect of stability; the decentred and asymmetrical positions and angles relate the mass of the galloping horse to the opening in the gate, accentuating the impression of powerful, implicit movement. The disquieting tension that builds up between the two patterns requires resolution.

Turning to the question of how viewpoint and perspective are used in *Church and Horse,* observation of the recession of the church's roof and of what can be seen of the gateway indicates that the line of sight is not far above the church's doorstep. It is low enough to place the viewer in a clearly diminutive position in regard to the façade of the church and the onrushing horse, but high enough that it does not correspond to the top of the yard. There could be – and indeed there is – something behind that sudden drop from view, though all that can be seen is a tombstone. The vantage point itself is situated on the central vertical axis of the painting, placing the viewer squarely in front of the church but off centre to the right in the gateway. Two systems of perspective, one- and two-point, are co-ordinated in the depth construction of the image and work much like counterpoint in music. With the single-point system, the vanishing point is located directly opposite the viewer, centred low on the church door but projected virtually far within or behind the building's suggested volume. Led deliberately, directly from its centred position up to the door, the viewer's eye is then abruptly denied access by the opaque plane of the church's façade rising in the advanced middle ground. Frustrated in its pursuit of distance, the eye is all but captured in the relatively shallow space between the gateposts and the doorstep. The double-point system, used to establish the angle and volume of the horse, is constructed from positions on the horizon line quite far to the right and left outside the picture. The heterogeneity of the horse's presentation detaches it from the static stability which governs the one-point system, conferring on it the power of coherent movement.

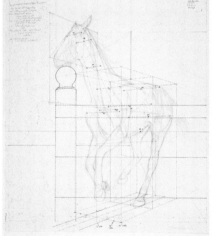

B.08

You are small, then, a child for at least the time you devote to experiencing this painting. From the open gateway, your life appears as a trajectory, a project to be invented as you confront and attempt to resolve the conflict between the choice that lies before you and an impending collision with your fate. There is no trodden pathway to the door of the church that dominates your view, bidding you welcome and forbidding you entry; the building's impassive exterior, though stable as a rock, cannot guarantee that once inside, you will indeed find the solace of belief and understanding you seek. You are left with the mere possibility that something worth caring about might be discovered within those whitened walls. And so it is that only in hope and with trepidation can you choose to pick your way across the overgrown yard, knowing all the while you may find nothing. The way is fraught with danger that comes, as the desire which animates your life, from you know not where. The dark horse of destiny races into your path, though you have not quite yet advanced to the momentous intersection. But it is only in the gloomy landscapes of anxiety that the envoy of fate surges forward, strangely noble in its unswerving resolve. There, it reveals the necessary, the inevitable conditions of your being. With acceptance of these, the hooves of doom take wing. Now you notice that the tombstone is as ambiguous as the rest of this world suffused with silver light. It is an image of death, but not necessarily an object of fear. If you wish, this image can give rise to a final confirmation, a moment of decision in which your hesitation at the gate is resolved.

B. CHURCH AND HORSE, 1964

Acrylic polymer emulsion on Masonite, XI/XLII
55.3 x 68.5 cm
The Montreal Museum of Fine Arts, purchase, Horsley and
Annie Townsend Bequest and anonymous donor

The Paintings

With the exception of *Kiss with Honda,* all the paintings produced by Alex Colville during the last decade figure in this exhibition. They are presented, each in its own relatively distinct display area, in the central gallery accessed directly from the entrance. Colville conceives of his paintings not as elements of a series, but as individual, coherent works which stand on their own. There are, however, more or less strong affinities among them. Based on the artist's approach to painting and his choice of subject matter, these affinities are like family resemblances – without destroying this daughter's or that son's personality, it is possible to say that she reminds you of this aunt, he of that cousin. The essential thing to keep in mind to avoid misunderstanding – and perhaps even insult – is that the similarities, the connections we trace out, are based on a clear recognition of the difference, the singularity, of each family member. Since serial development does not apply in Colville's case, the numerical sequence and presentation of the paintings does not follow their dates of production; but since family affinity clearly does apply, the works are assembled in loosely organized groups. This kind of presentation, like the experience of painting itself, requires interpretation and judgement which, in the last analysis, are subjective interventions. To some degree, the choice of the relationships used to form the clusters is therefore arbitrary. This is only one of many possible groupings of the paintings, each of which would reflect the life experiences, conditioned perceptions, biases and hopes of those responsible for the display.

The paintings are all executed with acrylic paint on high-grade Masonite panels finished on both sides. The panels are prepared with acrylic gesso applied to both sides and the edges to serve as a sealer as well as to provide a white ground for the paint. The gesso is laid on using relatively short, semicircular sweeps with a round-headed brush to avoid forming long parallel lines that might disrupt the visual unity of the paint surface; it is then sanded enough to remove irregularities without losing the "tooth" that enables it to bind paint to its surface. The gesso pattern can be seen through close-up examination of areas where the paint has been thinly applied.

The actual process of painting is relatively slow – Colville produces only two paintings a year and perhaps a serigraph – and involves minute attention to the details of paint application. Once the plan elaborated in his study drawings has been set out on the surface, he applies a thin wash of colour to appropriate areas, establishing an initial tone for the picture. The image is built up by layering and juxtaposing very small, thin brush strokes. Reminiscent of the small dots used by Seurat and Signac, Colville's strokes tend, however, to be less like small globules of paint than flat, rectangular touches of the brush that hold close to the surface of the work. Colour relationships are varied according to the requirements of the subject, sometimes by laying down different values of similar hues, as the lighter and darker blues used to compose sky, sometimes by bringing together complementary or primary and secondary colours to create an optical mix, as is found with the greens, browns and red oxide, which produce flesh tones, and the deep blue on a darker ground which functions as shade within the lighter greens of a tree. The overall tone of the painting is carefully monitored as the work progresses, and shifts away from the desired effect can necessitate a general reworking of the surface to bring the picture back into line. A picture is finished when the artist judges that nothing more is needed for it to correspond to his image-concept.

The frame for each painting is conceived, designed and built by Colville as a complement to the picture, and it is an integral aspect of the work's presentation.

The tide is still low in the harbour; its murky beige waters are quiet, rippling blue flashes of reflected summer sky. It is a bright, sun-lit day, hot. From the foreground of the picture, the prow of a boat sails directly towards the massive water-stained dock where it will soon seek to moor. The sailor's guiding hand, life-size and extremely close to the picture plane, enters the scene obliquely from the lower left-hand corner, as if pointing to the woman positioned high above on the dock. He wears a wristwatch, timeless under solar glare. Near the top of the ladder that climbs up the pier past the dark high-tide line to ground level, she stands, a small and solitary figure, waiting, one leg slightly advanced, the opposite arm held slightly forward, wearing a sleeveless white frock, hatless. Behind the vertical plane of the pier, which rises in the middle ground and continues with the regularly spaced posts upward into the sky, appear only the second storeys of houses and the leafy branches of trees spreading under a crystalline sky. There remain distances to be covered, intervals stretching across divisive waters and from hand to expectant heart. There is an unhurried, indolent breeze, hardly noticed as it flutters about the red sail, augmenting the anticipation of arrival.

The effect of *Arrival* on the viewer is due in large part to the ambiguity of the space between the sailor's hand and the woman on the wharf. The picture is constructed using contradictory sets of perceptual cues: the distance that remains to be covered by sailing into the depth of the picture is clearly indicated by the emphatic change of scale between the hand and the woman; but the boat and wharf are both tied into a strong geometric pattern that tends to compress the pictorial gap by pulling the wharf forward from the middle ground towards the picture plane. As the viewer's eye follows the angle indicated by the sailor's hand, the woman is perceived as both close and far away.

The surface pattern is a rhythmic, symmetrical grid based on "embedded" golden proportions, that is, the repetition of smaller examples of these proportions inside larger examples. The format is a horizontal golden rectangle. Any line can be cut at not only one, but two places to form golden sections depending upon the relative positions chosen for the long and short segments. If the top and bottom of *Arrival* are both segmented twice in this way and the four points produced paired vertically and joined, two vertical golden rectangles are formed something like the wings of a triptych. If these vertical golden rectangles are subsequently subdivided with their horizontal and vertical medians, each yields four more small golden rectangles. Drawing the vertical median of the original rectangle would then finish the vertical segmentation of the picture. These vertical divisions correspond to elements of the image – the right side of the mast, the posts rising above ground level and the right side of the ladder – effectively making the boat and wharf part of the

The . . . "Scaffie" boat enters Wolfville harbour – a woman stands on the wharf. The painting is small because the hand and the watch I felt could not be larger than life.

Alex Colville, "Remarks", November 1993

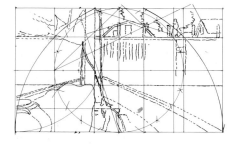

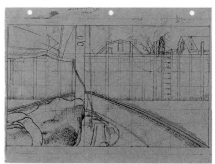

1.10

1. ARRIVAL, 1991

Acrylic polymer emulsion on Masonite
16.5 x 26.7 cm
Private collection

same pattern. If a value of 3 is given to the width of the smallest golden rectangles, from left to right the bands produce a rhythm of 3–3–2–median–2–3–3. From this symmetrical sequence, a square can be produced (3–2–median–2–3 or 5–median–5, because 10 is the proportional value of the height of the original rectangle), which confirms the stability of the pattern, and the proportions either way from the median to the sides, 2–3–3 or 5–3, add up to 8 and introduce the Fibonacci series.

When the grid is completed by segmenting the picture horizontally, a similar rigour in the correspondence of divisions to pictorial features is revealed. The horizontal median divides the tide stain on the wharf into equal bands. If both sides are segmented twice at the golden sections, paired horizontally and joined, the divisions produced correspond to the waterline and the high-tide line. Because the water's surface is part of the grid (the water and the wharf are of the same height), it tends to appear as a vertical rather than horizontal plane, thereby shortening the perceived distance between the sailor's hand and the woman.

The horizon is identical to the picture's horizontal median, and the vanishing point is located where the horizontal and vertical medians intersect. This places the viewer not far from the picture plane, to the right of and somewhat above the hand. Mirroring the virtual line by which the hand points towards the vanishing point is another line that starts in the top right-hand corner, follows the slant of the roof behind and to the side of the woman, and passes through the ladder by the woman's legs to the centre of the picture. Joined at the vanishing point, these two lines, which in other cases might be orthogonals, creating a strong impression of spatial recession, form a continuous diagonal from lower left to upper right. Used in this way, emphasizing the format and the picture plane, the mirrored lines pull the location of their junction – that is, the centre of the picture and the vanishing point – up to the surface of the image, again compressing the distance between hand and waiting woman. The vantage point offered to the spectator can then imply a triple, circular sequence of identities: the viewer is a sailor, the sailor is an artist, the artist is a viewer. All three are one and the same consciousness, looking, knowing, longing, desiring. The boat sails forward at a right angle to the picture plane and the wharf, but off centre to the left. It will need to pull to the right, following the sailor's hand, the painter's heart and the viewer's eye, to reach the ladder, the woman, home.

Involuntarily, my grip on the tiller tightens, the muscles across my back and shoulders, down my arms, tense in readiness. I am about to manoeuvre into docking position. I reach out from somewhere within, past and beyond my hand, to that place above the ladder where she stands in anticipation. I am not a camera. I am a pulse, a longing movement of the heart, a mind desiring, composing what my eye cannot see. This hand, as I glance towards her, is not in my field of vision but in my mind's eye. And there, as if embedded in unstable, shifting layers of my memory, appear other separations, other distances marked by the indomitable powers of the sea. Once, long ago, there stood *four figures on a wharf,* calm, stately women in the pale grief of white marble, draping themselves in mute expectancy and alabaster robes. How else could they address the horrible absence of those who were sent out across the sea, those who were gone to war? How else could they contain the recurring surge of anxiety but to dwell steadfast on the pier, enveloping their pain in gestures of immutable stone? Yet, were these figures really four, or were they for me all the same one – she who clothed herself with hope as she awaited my return from the waters of danger? Later, years after our reunion, the dock lingered on in my thoughts, an implanted image of our joy, of distance abolished; then this *woman on wharf* disrobed as I awaited her, a warmer figure against the threatening darkness of a calm but uneasy sea. Now, she waits once more. It is not as if the distance between us were over land. There, when separation occurs, it extends our closeness outward, stretching it to the limit, but never breaking our connection. The tie between us becomes more tenuous over the unpredictable sea, dissolving in our ancient fear of the disruptive, uncontrollable power of the waters. Now I am almost home. In a moment, after that brief instant when we see solitude in each other's eyes, distance will once again be abolished by her touch.

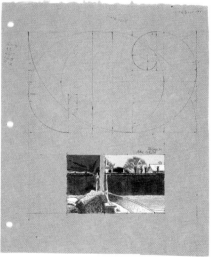

1.09

Looking down into water seems interesting to me. The boat (also depicted in "Boat and Bather") is a Drascombe Scaffie.

Alex Colville, "Remarks", November 1993

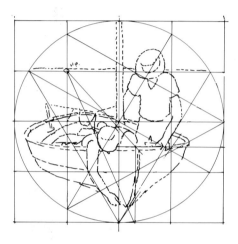

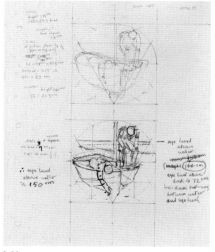

2.03

The bay is calm, the sun high, the light almost blinding in the still, crystal air. It is perhaps low tide – a horizontal bar of earthen yellow appears in the middle distance, emerging between parallel washes of rose-purple and light blue sea. Immobile, an olive green sailboat floats as if suspended slightly above the rippling surface, its prow close and turned at an obtuse angle to the picture plane, its mast dividing the upper part of the circular picture straight down the centre. No sail is visible. A woman wearing a yellow swimsuit and a white bathing cap lies on her stomach towards the front of the boat, her head over the edge, her right arm dangling beside the prow, her hand open in a noncommittal gesture to the water. Though her nose and cheeks can be made out, the features of her face cannot be discerned as she peers into what seems to be shallows close to an invisible shore. To her left in the boat stands a man. Intent on what she is doing, he bends forward at the shoulders; his head, concealed like his face under a white summer hat, is bowed in the direction of her gaze. His arms frame her position, extending her gesture backward across the interval which separates them. She seems unaware of him. He is lost in her total absorption. In the distance, on the horizon, lie the hazy mauve hills of the other shore.

The round format of *Looking Down* interrupts the movement of the eye as it follows the rise of the mast and the spread of the strong horizontals of the sea and the horizon, accentuating the closure of the picture and turning interest back into the flow of the shapes it presents to view. Inscribed within the circle is an equilateral triangle, one side running along the horizon. A point of the triangle rests at bottom centre, directly below the woman's fingertips and where the keel breaks water. The triangle's remaining sides are suggested by the man's forearm and the woman's dangling limb, thereby joining their gestures and gazes into a unified, concordant figure focussed on the object of their attention. Other linear connections reinforce what the triangle lays out, intensifying the complementary notions of autonomy and relatedness: the lemon-shaped oval of the boat sweeps around the woman and the man, bringing them physically together and suggesting that they are a couple; but the line in the form of a teardrop that curves across the woman's shoulder, down her arm and up the prow of the boat, turns her in on herself in a circular closure which echos that of the picture as a whole. The man's arms sketch out the possibility of an ellipse which would join him to her, but the form is broken by the imperious rise of the mast. The vantage point from which all this is seen is peculiar: located somewhat to the left and in front of the boat and at the height of the horizon, we too are *looking down* from a position – wading in the shallows, seated on a low dock, perhaps relaxing in a neighbouring boat – which is the counterpart of that occupied by the man. We too are involved in her, in their, gaze.

2. LOOKING DOWN, 1988

Acrylic polymer emulsion on Masonite
71.1 cm (diameter)
Royal Bank of Canada collection

Somehow we already know, you and I, what bond it is that brings this couple together while holding them apart. She peers into the translucent waters as we too have done. She is intent, very still, absorbed, as she looks through the rippling surface, attentive as her eyes explore the indeterminate, luminous depths of glimmering blues – turquoise and lapis lazuli. Minute things enter her view, rise, spin, dart away. Some drift suspended, some swim, swishing along invisible corridors, others crawl through their liquid milieu. Rays of light, glints of gold, dance to the flowing rhythms of the shifting current; bits of nameless things glitter. She watches and is no longer present on the boat. She is there, in the water, lost to him, lost to herself, lost within the confines of the infinite as once she was when, tossing her head back and *looking up,* she searched the ceiling of the universe. For the moment, she has gone somewhere else. She is where life gets its meaning, she is at one with what is. He knows. And so he waits, caring and solicitous, refusing the urge to wade into those depths to find her. It is her own place, and she will return. He holds his arms ready, feeling that closeness of love which requires distance.

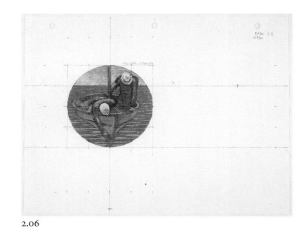

2.06

A woman wearing a yellow one-piece swimsuit and white bathing cap stands at relaxed attention, thigh-deep in the waters of the bay. Utterly still, engrossed in the patient watch of a sentinel, she towers monumentally above the viewer and the sea, close and at an acute angle to the picture plane, assurance and power concentrated in the generous, smoothly flowing contours of her sculptured body. She is looking out to sea, beyond the middle distance, perhaps to where a red-sailed boat passes at an angle almost parallel to hers. For the moment, the bather's view of the woman at the tiller, at least of her head and white hat, is obscured by the sail. The woman in the boat, too, gazes out to sea, apparently unaware she has entered the other's field of vision. Each of them is alone, these figures starkly isolated by golden highlights of summer sun. Each alone, these solitudes outlined against the hazy sky. But ever so still, the bather watches, and a bond forms between them in the soft lapping of the waters as she compresses the intervening space with her gaze.

The geometric structure and surface patterning of *Boat and Bather* focus our attention on what is essential in this picture – the abridged distance between the commanding, stable form of the bather and the diminutive shape of the sailor. The format of the work is a vertical rectangle composed of two horizontal golden rectangles placed one upon the other. The sail's peak touches the picture's upper framing edge at dead centre; if a line is dropped from this point to bisect the picture's surface, it intersects the mast just below the place where it rises from inside the boat, encounters the bather's left wrist, then runs down the edge of the highlight on her hand and on to the work's bottom edge. The horizon line – drawn mentally where the waters meet a vaporous bank of clouds – segments the rectangle to form a square of sky firmly seated on a relatively narrow rectangle of sea. The vanishing point is located where the vertical median meets the horizon, that is, the unseen place in the boat from which the mast rises, behind the bather's left hand just below the wrist. This arrangement rivets observer and boat together visually, shortening the distance between them, and anchors them both to the stable geometric structure of the image. The visual weighting of the image is, however, asymmetrical, suggesting movement from left to right. The bather occupies most of the right portion of the image, rising high from just below eye level and assuming the vertical stance of the whole format. In contrast, the boat is aligned with the horizon and is located to the left side of the picture, forming a directional vector and leaving much of the upper left to function as a vacant, negative area. Between these contrasting forms of stability and movement, there is a poetic unison of curves: the one-two beat of the swimsuit's line as it espouses the bather's buttocks flows into the twice-as-long reverberated arc of the crease along the boat's side; the drop of her right shoulder strap parallels the drape of the sail; the roundness of her bathing cap,

This painting owes something to the great Seurat in the National Gallery, London, but in mine both figures are female. The looming bather is not fragile.

Alex Colville, "Remarks", November 1993

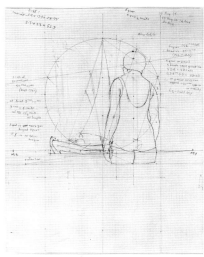

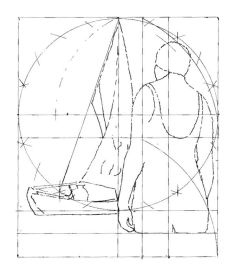

3.10

reflected on her back by the swoop of the bathing suit, is echoed by the sailor's hat. Both figures' shoulders belong to the same family of shapes, and these internal rhymes, like the similarity of sounds in song, draw the women together, declaring their proximity, suggesting their hidden identity.

We, though, spy this scene from a low, aqueous station, surreptitiously invading the woman's personal territory, prying with our stare into the distance she holds at her command. What is it that moves those of us who are male viewers to see as she sees? What drives our attempt to identify with her as we watch her watching? What is it that concerns us so? Most certainly, once we did sojourn those nine prescribed months enclosed in her waters, sharing the internal ebb and flow of her humours. Later, rising to the surface of the world, we clung to her side and began a long apprenticeship in affection. Now it matters little how far we have wandered from her breast, what different faces she might wear, or what roles she might play: we stand forever with this woman thigh-deep in the waters from which life emerges. And so we try our best to imagine what it is to stand here, watching as she watches the sailor pass through her world. Perhaps once more we can learn at her side. Hand relaxed, she views herself in that other person with the calm detachment of wisdom. In her quiet communion we discover what it is that lies in our own depths, extending beneath desire and difference. It is the identity, the oneness of being.

3.02

3. BOAT AND BATHER, 1984

Acrylic polymer emulsion on Masonite

66 x 53.4 cm

Private collection

This is the mouth of the Cornwallis River, near Wolfville, at low tide. The boat is a Boston Whaler. In a sense, it is about waiting (for the tide to come in?) – about nothing happening, but this does not imply impatience or boredom.

Alex Colville, "Remarks", November 1993

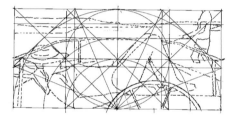

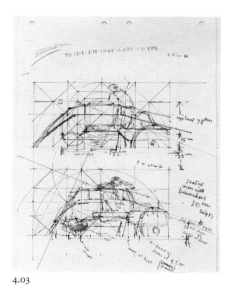

4.03

The viewer is on board a Boston Whaler, seated centre-aft just behind and to the left of the steering wheel, looking forward; the resulting line of sight corresponds to the craft's central axis, which runs at right angles from the picture plane and aims down the inlet until it meets the distant headland announcing open sea. The water level is low; the boat holds steady, bow tilted slightly upward but otherwise perfectly level, the stability of its horizontal symmetry suggesting that it might be temporarily grounded. In the foreground of the picture, a woman in a black bathing suit lies in sleepy languor parallel to the picture plane, distanced minimally from the viewer by the contracted space between her relaxed, gently curved arm and the steering wheel. Her feet lie flat on the raised surface of the forward deck, her bent legs form a restful double triangle. Head resting on a yellow pillow, canvas hat worn low over her eyes, she has withdrawn into herself to follow some indolent stream of wandering thought or perhaps to be lulled by the gentle flow of a hazy daydream. Her shadow holds her close to the deck. To the right, off the bow, a man stands in the shallows, his head deleted by the top edge of the picture. The space which separates him from the woman is puzzling: while it is compressed by his apparent position near the front of the boat, it is expanded by his relatively small scale and warped by a hidden bend in the cord which he holds taut. The man and woman are attached to each other, but the nature of their connection is not clear. His body language is also ambiguous: is he piloting the boat free of a mud bar, or is he acting as its mooring? Whatever the case, the work is not demanding; there is little tenseness in his arm, and he holds his body at ease, shadowless. At *low tide* there is a pause, a dispensation from exertion; all is comfort, calm and sensuous grace in the sumptuous warmth of the radiant sun.

The format and the implicit surface patterning of *Low Tide* reinforce the sentiments of ease and immanent, latent power centred in the voluptuous presence of the woman's supine body. Since the rectangular surface is exactly twice as wide as it is high, its vertical median line divides it into two contiguous squares. These, when bisected vertically, create another square located symmetrically within the first two. Further bisections, both horizontal and vertical, could then create smaller squares. This pattern is very stable and, capable of endless embedded subdivisions, recedes *inward,* as does the woman's mind, towards infinity. But the major divisions of the picture's surface nevertheless seem to be its vertical and horizontal medians. Divided into upper and lower sections – the former containing the sea, the man and the landmasses; the latter, the woman and the boat – the shapes above and below respond to each other: the contours of the woman's torso are of the same family as the lines of the earth forms; her body and knees fit visually into the form of the inlet; the man's arm and the cord bind him directly to that area of her anatomy

4. LOW TIDE, 1987

Acrylic polymer emulsion on Masonite
40 x 80 cm
Mr. R. Fraser Elliott collection

where her specific, female interiority resides. On the vertical median, which is identical with the viewer's central position, two important points are aligned: one in the sky, to which the somewhat upward-tilted handrails of the boat recede, and the other, a bit lower, the picture's vanishing point on the horizon where the headland juts into the sea. This curious discrepancy, as well as indicating the slight lift in the prow of the boat, seems to call the eye back towards the origin of the view within the boat and reinforces the comparison between the land forms surrounding the inlet and the recumbent shape of the woman. And, as if to confirm the connection of her body to the landscape, the vertical median identifies this feminine form as a headland which opens the way to a limitless sea.

The mood of this painting is tranquil, the atmosphere reposed, the attitude acquiescent. We viewers of the picture see first an external fact: the woman is lying down, apparently inactive, just letting time pass by. She waits. But gently, as we muse on this, the image offered to our view gives way to a reverie. The woman's supine body betrays no tension, harbours no anxiety. Outwardly, she can appear vulnerable, defenceless, because she knows what strength lies within. She is self-assured, at one with her surroundings. Identities, equations between things then come to mind, ancient equations, suggesting an equivalence between the woman's body and the land forms in the distance, between her inner life and the eternal ebb and flow of the sea. Deeply embedded in the past of humankind, this often-repeated identification of woman is now rejuvenated under our gaze; the image we see here is a threshold, a doorway through which we can enter into contact with the immanent, life-giving and restorative powers of nature. Some of us might call the external splendour of this woman's immanence her beauty. Touched by it, directed, we seek the infinite already present in our souls.

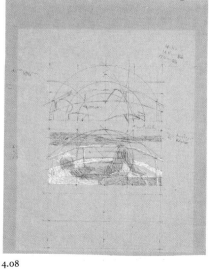

4.08

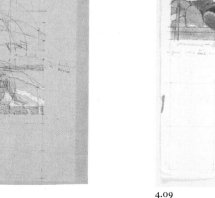

4.09

Calm, the waters' surface softly swells, and opalescent ribbons undulate, shift, breathe, iridescent with the hues of mother-of-pearl; near the boulder-lined shore, they fragment, rippling and reflecting the dark brown tones of the stone. In the centre of the picture, at an angle somewhat off the diagonal, a woman wearing a blue bathing suit floats on her back, head to the lower left. The mass of her body is submerged in the undisturbed opaque water which espouses her form; barely rising above the surface, only the front of the woman's swim cap, face and torso, a small portion of her right hand, thigh and knee, and the toes of her left foot are visible. Through their forms and distribution, these body shapes, emerging motionless, resemble a low-lying archipelago, and their spacing at rhythmic intervals, reminiscent of the distances used to place stones in Japanese gardens, implies a quiet harmony between the woman and the waters. The viewer, located in line with the woman's bathing cap, looks down on the scene, but from a vantage point not far above the surface, from a boat, possibly, or standing in the water.

The geometric structure of this painting is an application of Le Corbusier's Modulor and the Fibonacci series. The Modulor grid, when traced out over the image, can be seen to fit the length of the woman's body in such a way that her head corresponds to a width with a value of 3, and the rectangle that frames her hand, leg, knee and toes, a value of 5. At both ends of the Modulor, the artist has added two rectangles, seen in the painting as areas of unoccupied water and shore, each with a value of 5. The angle at which the woman floats can be obtained by segmenting the vertical framing edges, on the right at their upper and on the left, their lower golden sections, and joining them with an oblique line. This slanted transversal, though in keeping with the regulated vertical and horizontal grid, mathematical series, and golden sections, introduces a perfectly balanced and counterbalanced tilt, an arrested implicit movement, into the structure of the image.

Do you know how to float? The water is naturally buoyant and it attempts to support your torso and limbs but, fluid, it slips away to the sides, enveloping you as it lets you sink. You arch your back slightly, you raise one arm ever so slowly, letting it flow as if it too were liquid, you adjust the angle of your leg, shifting the distribution of your weight until you feel an internal balance, the lift of the waters with which you have become one. The essence of floating is internal, the result of a sensitivity to the play of energies within your body and of a disciplined response, a gentle, smooth interior control which aims not at domination, but at collaboration with your immediate surroundings. The issue is of crucial importance and identical with love: if your intervention is too aggressive or if you lapse into total passivity, you will sink. The implications are wide: like this woman, our culture needs to float

The woman floats calmly far out from a shadowed sandstone cliff.

Alex Colville, "Remarks", November 1993

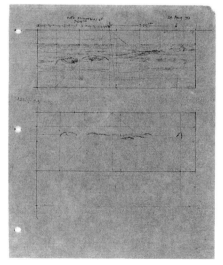

5.02

on the surface which divides the elements, to work with and not against the forces of nature; like this woman, you and I need the understanding and self-discipline to tap into the energetic flow that animates the world around us rather than exploit it as if we could claim it as a possession. An ancient image comes to mind, that of Turtle rising to the surface of the primordial waters, bearing on its back the mud that created the land and the life with which it is inhabited. Turtle floats on the surface, joining in perfect equilibrium the life-giving waters and the air we breathe, you and I.

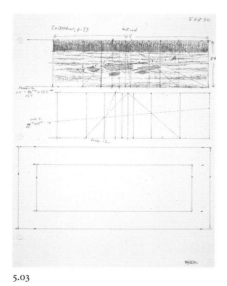

5.03

5. FLOATING WOMAN, 1990

Acrylic polymer emulsion on Masonite
26.7 x 86.4 cm
Private collection

Weathered to a soft grey, a wooden diving board cuts diagonally from the lower right towards the upper left corner of the picture, receding obliquely from the picture plane into the middle foreground. It is propped up on heavy wooden beams, likewise discoloured by time, which run at an angle from the bottom left of the image to a low position on the right vertical edge. The beams seem to be a guardrail at the top of a dock or sea wall, for far below stretches a calm expanse of muddy, rippling water, retreating past marshy lowlands tinted the light greens and pale yellows of lush grasses and sedges until it encounters distant dusky hills ranged along the horizon. A woman in a horizontally striped bathing suit – slate grey, yellow and brick orange – lies face down on the diving board, her feet above the juncture of the board and the rail, her head jutting over the end and overlapping the horizon line. Her left arm hangs straight down, a metal bracelet dangling at her wrist. Although projected over the indeterminate void which distances her from the surface of the inlet, like the water below she lies quietly in the strong sunlight, apparently at ease, tranquilly ruminating. If she is peering downward, it is unlikely that she can be absorbed by looking into the opaque, silt-tinged waters; suspended in midair, thrust into space like a projectile, arm and bracelet pulled towards the sea, it is more likely that she is exploring the vertiginous space which separates her from the surface… as long as she does not dive.

Woman on Diving Board is emotionally centred on the absence of an articulated close middle ground which would provide the viewer's eye with a transition between the woman and the sea. Instead, there is empty air, an invisible presence marked by the perpendicular drop of the woman's arm and bracelet. Much of the effect is also due to the angular construction of the image. The position of the diving board exploits the implicit, unimpeded movement of the diagonal running from bottom right to top left to project the woman into the region of the void. The format of the work is a root-3 rectangle, that is, one in which the diagonal, measuring exactly twice the height of the rectangle, forms angles of 30 and 60 degrees at the corners. The centre of the rectangle, located by dividing it into quadrants, falls on the upper visible edge of the diving board just below the woman's thigh. A square equal in width to the rectangle's height is centred in the rectangle; its vertical edges run along the left side of the woman's arm and shoulder on one side and through her left foot and heel on the other. Inside the square is inscribed a circle with a diameter equal to the square's width, and this in turn is inscribed with a hexagon which touches the tip of the woman's hand and the diving board at her armpit and just below the arch of her left foot. When two supplementary circles of the same diameter are centred on the midpoints of the vertical sides of the square, they cut the vertical framing edges at the horizon line and at the point where the

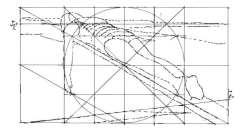

6. WOMAN ON DIVING BOARD, 1989

Acrylic polymer emulsion on Masonite
48 x 83.1 cm
Private collection

top right edge of the diving board and the closer edge of the guardrail intersect. A horizontal line joins the tips of the woman's fingers and her toes, forming with her body a right triangle which strengthens the effect of the board's strong diagonal.

An oblique perspective with two vanishing points situated outside the image to right and left on extensions of the high horizon line was used along with a strong contrast of scale to produce the picture's forceful impression of indeterminate depth. The station point leads to the horizon line just above where the woman's bathing suit curves up from the small of her back, objectively placing the viewer on the wharf and subjectively identifying the viewer with the projection of the woman's body over the void.

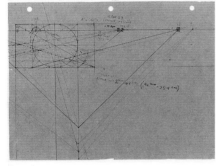

6.02

Deprived as we are of her face, her eyes and her thoughts, there is not much we can know about this woman. What we can dwell on is what we can see: her position on the board, her gesture, her attitude in space. She soars immobile over the void, tranquil, fearless, though she is clearly at an edge, a place of decision. For the time being her activity is suspended, and the moment stretches into duration, a fullness of presence; in her prone form is effected a juncture of the two primary movements of human awareness – that which delves inward, seeking the centre of the self, and that which extends outward, trying to achieve a relationship with whatever else there is or might be. At this juncture, immanence and transcendence are the same: the woman's still body and pendulous arm aim at the void, her depths are sounded and resound in the waters her attitude resembles, and the waters tell us of the woman's heart. If, as we observe her there, basking in the sun, we allow ourselves to feel as she feels, to see with her eyes, we also might find that how we image ourselves inside is a construction built of the things we care about outside and, in all of that, the focal point is the return of our gaze by those we love. At the juncture is a fundamental choice, a plunge, a leap outside the self into the unknown world of the other. It seems this choice cannot be made with the reassurances of reason alone, but only when we open ourselves to the hope that wells up within, from the centre of our being, from the place where existence springs, flowing forever outward and ebbing forever back towards its source within.

The day has just begun, or perhaps reached its end, in the soft grey gloom which blankets the shore and submerges the distant trees in depths, darker yet, of impenetrable mystery. From the left foreground a figure advances on the orange rock-strewn littoral, carrying on its shoulders an inverted canoe which glows, lustrous, white, as the sweep of its curved form arches gracefully into the twilight scene. The figure wears khaki slacks, which outline the full buttocks as the left leg steps forward, and a pullover, which is dark, like the space being traversed. The horizontal stripes of the sweater curve around its wearer's body, countering and harmonizing with the arc of the water as it meets the shore and with the flowing lines of the canoe as it greets the darkness. The figure's head, thrust inside the canoe in front of the seat, cannot be seen, but the right hand clutching the canoe's wooden trim is well enough illuminated to reveal that the grip is firm. For the moment, the functions of passenger and conveyance have been reversed: it is the means of transportation that is being transported, relieved of its role in the carrying-across, the portage into, or out of, day. Partially blinded by the canoe, the person carrying it cannot see far into the transitional gloom. There are two flat rocks on the ground immediately ahead that will have to be side-stepped in order to avoid stumbling. On the opposite shore, approximately at eye level, a zone of light glimmers, faintly illuminating the branches and tree trunks of the spectral woods beyond.

The mental and emotional focus of *White Canoe* is the relationship between the generalized figure of a human being and the conditions that govern its voyage, its quest, at the edge of night. The situation is embodied in the structure of the picture: the strong, flowing recession of the canoe and the implicit movement of the figure as they aim obliquely into the sombre depths of the scene are anchored to the picture plane by a complex geometric pattern that, through the relationships it creates on the painting's surface, constrains or weighs down the work of portage.

The vertical rectangular format of *White Canoe* consists of two equal golden rectangles, one on top of the other, their conjunction tracing the horizontal median. A square with sides equal to the width of the painting is centred top to bottom, its corners joined by diagonals. Around the painting's centre point (which is also the centre of the square) two concentric circles are inscribed, with radii half the height of the painting and half its width. The four points created by the intersection of the smaller circle and the diagonals of the square are joined to form a smaller square, which tightly frames the human figure and the canoe: the right edge runs down the front of the canoe; the left runs along the left arm of the figure; the top includes the canoe's brown trim; and the bottom passes along the creases of the slacks, just below the buttocks. Based on this inner square, two systems of proportions, vertical and horizontal, are generated. The distance to the edge of the painting above and

I got this Kevlow canoe, moulded from a Chestnut canoe, from my friend Ned Franks, author of a book on canoeing. The figure may be male or female; this seems to be a feature of contemporary life.

Alex Colville, "Remarks", November 1993

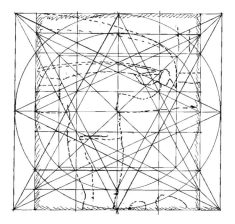

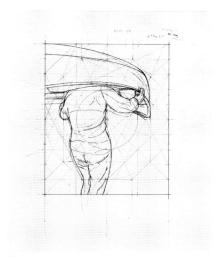

7.04

below this square is twice as great as that from its left and right sides to the sides of the painting. Vertically, this 2-to-1 proportion tends to compress the square, squeezing the canoe down on the figure's body. If the distance from the sides of the inner square to the sides of the picture is assigned a value of 2, then, on the lateral axis, the distance from the right framing edge to the front edge of the canoe, to the middle of the picture, to the point where the outer side of the left leg intersects the bottom edge of the inner square, to the left arm, to the left edge of the painting would be expressed proportionally (from right to left) as: 2–5–3–2–2. The 3 and 5 can be recombined to form an 8, the subsequent number in the Fibonacci series. Of particular interest is the space between the figure's left leg and the left edge of the picture: with a value equivalent to the distance from the top of the inner square to the edge of the painting, it seems to push the leg forward. The figure stands in the left half of the picture, against the vertical dividing line. This asymmetry is counterbalanced by the right arm and the front of the canoe as they stretch across the centre of the picture into the tenuous presence of night.

As we fall in line behind this everyman or -woman, we realize that we are either too early in the dawn to know the purposes of the day that lies ahead or too soon in the dusk to know what mysteries may be confronted in the night. We see at once that the figure's view is blocked by its burden; we share in the opacity that obscures its advance. Yet, we know there must be a purpose, as we do on the eve of any enterprise requiring care. The figure moves with deliberation, scanning the rock-strewn shore immediately ahead, choosing steps one by one, shifting weight a bit when necessary to restore the canoe's balance, from time to time readjusting its heading. The canoe-bearer envisions and aims at an unseen destination, mentally projects a tentative map that outlines the efforts and decisions to be made. Each meticulous step taken under the weight of the canoe acquires its meaning from its position on the map: side steps, corrective reorientations, even mistaken turns can lead to revisions of the map, but each and every movement belongs to the project. Is this portage not an image of our life, of the moment we realize that the means used to help us progress along the way are as dense with bearing, with significance, as the end to be attained? Is this portage not an accumulation of small practical decisions, a discovery that the path we tread is as integral to our being as the destination we project, that the way and the purpose, requiring each other, together give us our meaning, our individual passports for the journey at hand? It is. And our steps are lit by the faint but certain light of hope which penetrates the double-edged night.

7.03

7. WHITE CANOE, 1987

Acrylic polymer emulsion on Masonite

70.75 x 56.6 cm

Private collection

Doing nothing is a necessary pre-requisite to thinking. Also, I have known couples who rarely spoke to each other but each spoke to their dog, who became a link – like the new link to Prince Edward Island.

Alex Colville, "Remarks", November 1993

They are sitting at slight angles to each other on the verandah, she in her yellow striped bathing suit, he in his black boxer swimsuit and dark loafers. Out there, past the white grid of uprights and window frames, the heat of day shimmers in the still air; the lawn between the house and the shore is verdant under the golden sun, and across the bay the distant headland emerges from the luminescent atmosphere like a blue-grey phantom. Tranquillity pervades the verandah as well. Seated on a wooden bench, the woman leans forward, her right elbow on her leg, as if to catch a bit more light on the paper she is reading. It is an advertisement or special flyer – we can read the word "sale" where the page begins to curve upward to form a linear silhouette that repeats the shape of the end of the canoe upturned on the lawn. She is looking to see what bargains might be interesting, but she is taking it real easy. He is too, seated on his canvas-and-wood director's chair, legs crossed, hands behind his head, as if there were nothing to do but look out to sea. He is thinking, perhaps, of something specific, but more probably from his relaxed attitude, he is letting his mind wander in musings as hazy as the day. Like the sleeping dog, the woman and man have temporarily taken a holiday from their tasks and duties; they are secure, carefree, abandoned to the warmth of the day. It is a suspended moment: neither the couple nor the interlopers who witness the intimacy of this scene from behind can read the time behind the reflective crystal of the man's wristwatch.

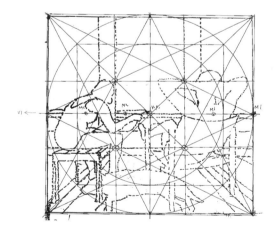

Although they are immersed in their respective interior worlds, the woman and the man seem nevertheless to be present to each other on another level of feeling, that of an implicit mutual awareness, a firmly grounded, nonreflexive attitude of attention, an unwavering state of mutual care. The sentiment that they share this depth of companionship is keyed to the geometric structure of the painting by the use of oblique two-point perspective to present his chair, in contrast to the frontal centralized perspective employed for her seat and the verandah itself. His chair is turned slightly towards hers, and she sits at an angle on hers, as if the positions were unconsciously arranged to permit easy eye contact and conversation. The vanishing points for his chair are located fairly far outside the picture to the right and closer in to the framing edge on the left. The vanishing point for hers and the verandah is located just under the tip of the newspaper near the point where the distant headland slopes down behind the horizontal window frame. She leans out of the stable coherence of her position, ready at any moment to shift into renewed personal interaction.

They have been together long enough now to have discovered that memory inhabits the body as well as the mind. All of the events they have shared – their meeting, his departure, her waiting, his return, their loving – all they have done and all that has

8. VERANDAH, 1983

Acrylic polymer emulsion on Masonite
80 x 80 cm
Private collection

befallen them has shaped how they think, how they feel, how they move. Over the years, sharing, once a tender exchange between the two, has somehow become a sentiment which makes their being one: he sees with her eyes, she foresees what he will think; he feels with her heart, she loves with his desire. They both know of painful, immeasurable distances and of joyous proximities. From within, they touch. The care is unspoken.

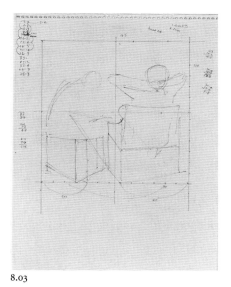

8.03

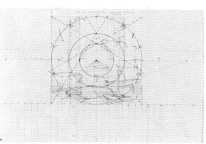

8.06

Profiled against a radiant sky glowing subtle tints of cobalt, tender green, pink and mauve, steel beams and girders delineate the close middle ground of *Couple on Bridge,* segmenting the picture into an asymmetrical though visually stable pattern of rectangles, triangles and squares. Rising from the light blue and green rippling waters, a concrete footing supports the bridge at the left framing edge and indicates by the angled recession of its upper and lower edges the central position of the vanishing point on the shore of the green landmass in the distance. To the top and right sides of the picture, the beams extend outward with no end angles or supports; it is clear that only a selected part of a larger scene is being presented. But as shown, the bridge nevertheless floats as if it were suspended in thin air. The viewer is stationed at the horizontal centre of the image, somewhat above the water level and below the bridge, perhaps in a boat. A casually dressed couple of mature age stands on the bridge, she in line with the viewer, he somewhat to the right. She is seen frontally, one wrist draped over the bridge's railing; her other arm leans on the rail with bent elbow, her hand cupping her chin. Her gaze is directed not at the man, but outward into the space above the viewer. Her stance and facial expression distance her somewhat from the man: they betray not rejection, but a kind of resignation to the inevitable, a bemused tolerance. She listens abstractedly, for he, alert, turned half away from the viewer, looking at his partner and gesturing emphatically, is not simply talking. He is expounding some idea that has captivated his mind. Once again.

Both Le Corbusier's Modulor and the Fibonacci series of proportional measurements underlie the graceful, dynamic balance of *Couple on Bridge.* If the top edge of the horizontal beam that establishes road level on the bridge is used to segment the square-format picture into two rectangles, the upper one can be subdivided into a version of the Modulor pattern which is truncated on the right side in accordance with the overall proportions of the image. The key position in the Modulor known as the place of the right angle is located in the picture at the point where the top edge of the angled girder closest to the viewer encounters the top framing edge slightly right of centre and in line with the woman's left side. The angle formed where this girder meets the beam at road level is 50 degrees, exactly that required by the Modulor construction. The virtual verticals that line up with both the woman's and the man's left sides pertain to the same construction and tie the figures tightly to the structure of the bridge, she positioned directly on the vertical centre line and he off centre to the right. His gesturing arm is directed to the woman's head, which is located just below the centre point of this upper rectangle. The lower rectangle is divided into two equal parts by the horizon line, and the vanishing point is located in the centre, directly below the woman. Taken in their entirety, the dimensions of the picture break down to the proportions of the Fibonacci series as follows: on the

Marilyn Burnett has noticed that a drawing for this painting is called "Intractable Muse". The exchange takes place in an environment which is unaffected.

Alex Colville, "Remarks", November 1993

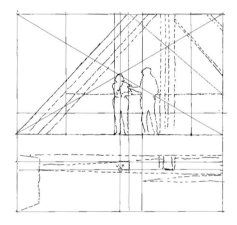

9.09

9.10

horizontal, 21 inches from the left edge to the virtual line dropping along the man's left side, 5 inches from there to the right side of the foremost vertical girder, and 8 inches to the right framing edge, making a total of 34 inches; on the vertical, 13 inches from the bottom framing edge to road level and 21 inches from road level to the top framing edge, again a total of 34 inches.

As unshakable as the bridge's girders, the woman is at the picture's physical, geometric, rhythmic and psychological heart. It is to this interior site that the man's gesture opens, claiming his place at the centre.

I see the couple standing above as my rowboat drifts slowly towards the bridge, rocking gently. The rippling waters slip easily to the sides, whispering opalescent and emerald memories of the depths. I am almost asleep, eyes half-closed in the luminosity of this day. In my reverie, the woman appears, self-contained, rapt in a bemused absence, opaque, sufficient unto herself. My attention shifts and, for this present moment, it is only the man who concerns me. His plight is that he needs her, and in this I discover a deep affinity, a complicity with those of my unquiet sex who are born wombless, knowing ourselves incapable of gestating life, of giving birth. For that, we clearly need her. But also, it seems, she is required for more. We men have little other with which to create, to establish the new, than what happens in our minds. So the man on the bridge, like me, like all other men, must endure on his own the headache of Zeus: *After he consumed Metis, the pain in Zeus' head became terrible. Then, when Hephaestus struck him on the temple, Athena, goddess of the arts, of cities, of war and of wisdom, sprang directly from his head, fully clothed and armed.* My sombre musings slip like the deep waters beyond: Can we men conceive anything, be it only in our heads, if we are denied a woman's gaze?

9. COUPLE ON BRIDGE, 1992

Acrylic polymer emulsion on Masonite
86.4 x 86.4 cm
Private collection

Yellowed grasses jut in scattered clumps through the thin covering of snow that has blanketed the shooting range; in the background a dark stand of winter trees rises opaque, a gloomy tapestry of trunks and branches. The snow has sifted in light patches onto the gravelly ground of the open shed which houses the shooters' firing stations; like the snow, daylight filters horizontally, soft, glowing, into the shed from the left. In stall 14, separated from the viewer by an upright post in the foreground, stand two men, the closer and younger taking aim with a target pistol, the slightly more distant and elder watching the target area with binoculars. Both men occupy the right side of the image, and both look to the left on the same line of sight, that determined by the pointing of the pistol. The young man, feet apart, stands parallel to the picture plane, one hand in his pocket, the other outstretched, gripping the pistol. His hair flows back from his brightly illuminated brow and face, his jaw is set, his lips are tight, his gaze intent. His total attention flows into his aim. He grips the trigger. The older man is just as preoccupied, but by a different concern. He stands beside and somewhat behind the youth, at a right angle to the picture plane, uplifted arms holding binoculars, lower face and hands radiant, waiting for the shot to fire. Intently, he scrutinizes the target area, ready to examine the results of the young man's aim, to comment, to suggest alternatives, to teach. For the time being, he is entirely focussed by what happens over the young man's shoulder. The yellow hues of the grasses, the lining of the youth's jacket and the man's sports coat warm both the crisp white of snow and shirt and the sombre tints of the woods as the young man tightens his grip slowly. You catch sight of this ritual from the neighbouring stall. A discreet glance is enough for you and me to grasp the fragile weight of the moment.

If a circle is inscribed in the square chosen as the format for *Target Shooting*, the arc produced at the top intersects the gun near the youth's trigger finger and the older man's face where he peers into the binoculars, signalling and distilling the essential relationship portrayed in the work by the horizontal alignment and directionality of the binoculars, the youth's eyes and the sighting level of the pistol. The top edge of the square produced by joining the points where this circle intersects the work's diagonals corresponds to eye level – the horizon line – and is situated just below the youth's and man's sight line, running through the middle of the youth's pistol hand and chin to go on across the man's mouth and below his ear. The vanishing point is located where the young man's firmly set chin curves upward towards his ear and encounters his highlighted neck. If the picture is divided by its vertical median, the line runs down the youth's right side and crowds both men together in the right half of the scene; from this area they move virtually by pointing through the relative emptiness of the left side towards a target which cannot be seen. The viewer, located

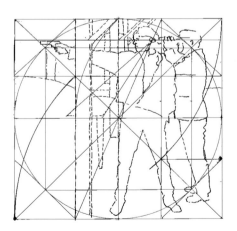

10. TARGET SHOOTING, 1990

Acrylic polymer emulsion on Masonite
80 x 80 cm
Private collection

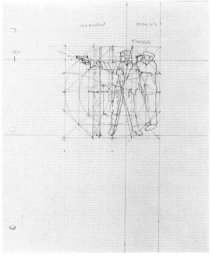

10.05

on the same side as the men, just below their sight line, looks up slightly in order to identify with what they are doing and to participate in their alignment with the target.

Was that a slight shudder of fear that ran through us as we noticed murderous potential in the paramilitary stance of the men beside us? I, for my part, want now to pause and take some distance, for there is an ominous weight here. We could, I know, simply shrug off this vague fear because it is after all just *target* shooting, but there is more to it than that. Born from the violence of war and the hunt, it is hard for guns to be entirely innocent: an aura of pain and destruction looms menacingly out of their past; forebodings of coercion and death accompany their appearance. Distance and control are intrinsic elements of the issue: guns hit out at their target, placing the gunner in a position of physical and mental domination. In this context, binoculars are the pistol's double; they likewise reach out, contact and provide strategic information while protecting the observer from exposure. These are fearful things, the gun and the binoculars, but here, deliberately given an abstract target, they seem to become both tools and images of the necessary, difficult apprenticeship in the art of fixing one's aims, of setting self-imposed goals. The youth chooses a target, adjusts his aim until he and the target are one. Then, relaxed in his certitude, he slowly squeezes the trigger and fires. There is a mentor behind the youth providing counsel, and whether he be father or instructor, he is potentially as dangerous as the instruments with which he imparts a tradition. See how he stands, how he holds himself close and yet far away from the youth? It seems to me – and I hope you can agree – that the urgency that weighs upon us as we think on this is the realization that teaching, that all forms of guidance, of sharing our collective ways and personal experiences, are precariously balanced on an edge that separates love and violence. The burden is therefore very fragile and can be carried only with the greatest of care. The faces of both the youth and the older man are suffused with light as each envisions the target.

Facing left, a nude woman stands in the immediate foreground of the picture at the top of a flight of stairs, her image truncated at the level of her chin and calves by the work's top and bottom framing edges respectively. She is holding a Smith and Wesson Body Guard revolver in her left hand, index finger curled over the trigger. Light emanating from an invisible source to the left bathes her body, accentuating its round, full contours with strong highlights and warm shades. Behind her, the rectilinear cavity of a dark stairwell plunges to the brightly illuminated hall below, where little can be seen but rugs on the hardwood floor and perhaps a table leg. Occupying the space from the foreground to the middle ground, the dim stairwell is like an upturned box which closes the space located at and above eye level upon the statuesque form of the woman, framing and capturing her in its rigorous straight lines and flat planes, only to open upon the bright but mysterious floor area which slides out of sight at the bottom of the stairs. The woman is attentive, her body at ease but ready to respond. She is in control. We listen with her, very carefully, for even a slight sound from below.

Woman with Revolver is composed much like a Classical Greek play: what is actually seen on stage, incomplete in itself, is supplemented by the chorus's comments upon offstage events to complete the narrative. The difference with *Woman with Revolver* is that the critical information about what is missing is only evoked or suggested in the form of various possibilities, and these remain irremediably ambiguous. However, far from being rationally objective about the alternatives, the situation depicted is emotionally charged, and this seems to be due, at least largely, to the tense contrasts used in the presentation of the subject matter. The rectangular format of the picture is based on two squares placed one above the other, the virtual line of their junction running just above the baseboard on the back wall of the stairwell. The upper square contains mainly the closed top of the well, and the lower, the stairs and floor below. The woman's figure joins the two. The strong verticality thus established accentuates both the plunging view down the stairs and the marked absence, on the one hand, of the woman's head and therefore of her facial expression, and on the other, of what occupies the space extending from the lower hallway. Occupying the right half of the picture in the extreme foreground, the torso of the woman towers over the stairwell, the generous, curved contours of her body closing her in upon herself; her undeniably strong, life-affirmative flesh stands out against the dim, rigid enclosure of the stairwell and dominates the brightly lit area of floor below, which opens to the space hidden from view. The vanishing point is located at the horizontal centre of the image at the level of the woman's diaphragm. Seeing the scene from an eye level considerably lower than the woman's, and with access to the stairs cut off by her body and bent knee, the viewer has little choice but

The Smith and Wesson revolver depicted is known as the "Body Guard Airweight." It is part alloy, .38 calibre, 5-shot cylinder. The woman is of course not a helpless creature.

Alex Colville, "Remarks", November 1993

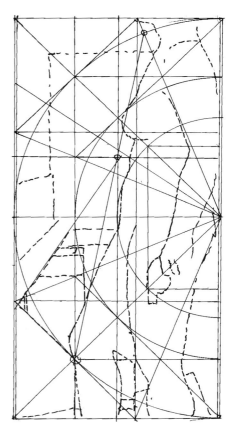

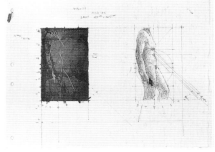

11.06

to adopt a position of visual and emotional dependency upon the woman. She holds the Body Guard in easy readiness.

Now, in the hushed shades of midnight, terror stirs secretly, unrecognized, in the marrow of her bones. Violence lurks here, muffled in the deep blue and gold of the caged stairs; in dead silence anxiety rumbles and roars, twisting in her stomach as it clutches for her heart. Dread pervades her thoughts, making her one with all the violated, and she knows instinctively what she must know. Disaster threatens, and the guardian of her body, small, lightweight, carefully shaped, nestles in her grip as if it were part of her hand, powerful and deadly as the claws of a lioness. Secure, her vulnerability protected, she relaxes to stay prepared. The terror recedes, the rage is controlled, and she will do what she must do for her body and for her home. Now, in the quiet safety of midnight, there is the murmur of an age-old debate. Is it true, as Jean-Jacques Rousseau held, that it is society which instigates violence; is it really true that, if left in a state of nature, human beings would prove to be essentially good? The Marquis de Sade thought the contrary: if given back to nature without constraints, human beings would become depraved beasts and nature would not care; society and culture exist to frame and to channel violence. When, after suffering the wickedest of torments, Justine finally escapes from her vile captors and flees from the castle, she is struck dead by lightning. To the degree that existence involves change, violence underlies all things and processes like the lava seething deep below the volcano. Neither good nor bad in itself, it is there, a function of nature. The light weight of the revolver in the woman's hand is all it takes to reveal an ethical difference.

11.09

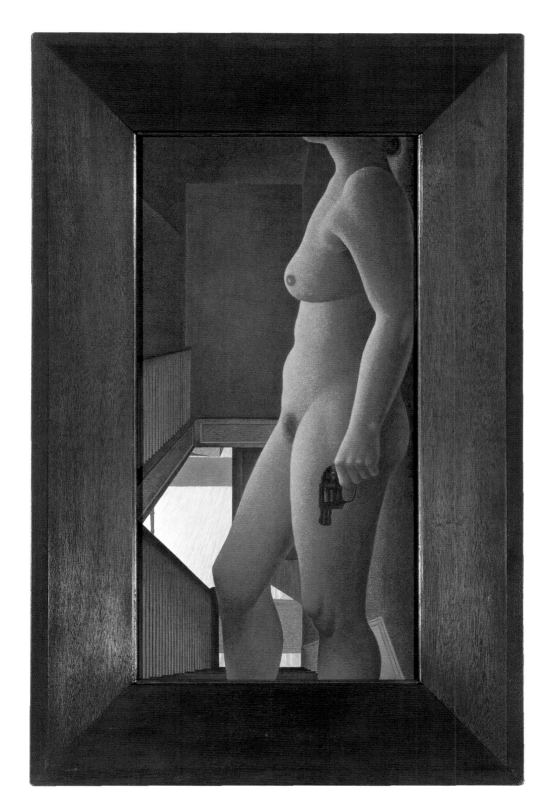

11. WOMAN WITH REVOLVER, 1987

Acrylic polymer emulsion on Masonite
56.5 x 28.2 cm
Mira Godard collection

Part of the idea for this came from seeing a stone fragment, leg and feet, Greek, I think 6th century B.C. in the Metropolitan Museum. The dog (now gone) and cat (now eighteen) got on well with each other and the human represented.

Alex Colville, "Remarks", November 1993

The room where the three of them – dog, cat, person – are grouped is probably the kitchen or perhaps the pantry. All three face a white freestanding radiator to the left of the picture. Rectangular brick red tiles run in staggered courses across the bottom of the picture but recede little farther than the radiator before they reach the white baseboard, door casing and olive green walls which rise in the middle ground. The brown door stands ajar, revealing a continuation of the tile floor into what might be a corridor leading to the left and another white wall which blocks the view of what might be beyond. A white saucer and a black bowl with a white interior have been placed in front of the radiator. Closest and parallel to the picture plane, the dog stands before the bowl, her head lifted in wary, distrustful attention. Her pelt is rich, black as anthracite highlighted with warm brown and a sheen of blue-grey. Her ears hang but with a suggestion of tenseness, her brown eyes have rolled to the side, and their black pupils are fixed steadily on the position of the viewer. The length of her body stretches almost the whole width of the picture, as if protecting the cat and the person. Crouched at the other side of the dog's front legs, the tabby cat eats from the saucer, unaware or unconcerned that it is being observed. Slightly farther away, between the doorway and the dog's hind legs, stand the bare, vulnerable feet and naked legs of the person. No more is visible. The dog watches, prepared for trouble. She is in charge.

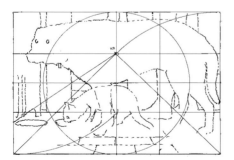

Shallow in depth but flowing laterally, the spatial geometry used in this picture emphasizes the ordered grouping of the figures in compressed layers and the protective function of the dog. The format is a root-2 rectangle. If the original square from which the rectangle is generated is placed on the left side, the perpendicular corresponds to the front of the person's advanced leg; if the original square is located on the right side, the perpendicular corresponds to the edge of the door casing behind the cat's head. This produces, in conjunction with the vertical median on which the vanishing point falls, a strong laterally symmetrical grid. The figures are layered across this grid in accord with three principal horizontal lines: the median, the line where the tile floor meets the wall, and the viewer's eye level, which runs just above the dog's nostrils and along the length of her body. Eye level is the same distance down from the top of the picture as the line where the floor meets the walls is up from the bottom edge. This vertical linear symmetry contrasts expressively with the massing of the figures: the dog's dark bulk in the upper half of the image hovers protectively over the cat and the person's feet. As if to confirm the dog's defensive role, the intruder's eyes are drawn to the vanishing point, in the dog's powerful chest, just behind her shoulder.

12. CAT AND DOG, 1986

Acrylic polymer emulsion on Masonite
28.2 x 40 cm
Courtesy of Deloitte & Touche Inc. (from the Central Guaranty Trust Collection)

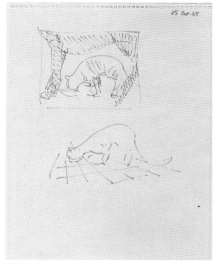

12.02

I am frozen in place by her stare. At my approach, her first startled instant of surprise vanished as she arrested the turn of her head and, cautioning, establishing her territory, fixed those eyes on me. Her hackles still lie flat to her neck and back; she has not yet decided what to do; she holds her ground, assesses the situation. The weight of this pause is enough to affirm that there will be no aggression if I can show that I am not an aggressor. But I need time, time to prove with my body what my mind cannot convincingly say, attentive time, for we are so radically different, she and I. Now, in this confined space, we are both pinned to the spot by a mutual animal awareness of our presence. She scans me with acute accuracy, learning my intentions, my attitudes, my real name, as I attempt to relax; through the glare in her eyes she observes and analyzes the minute changes of tension I display as my fear turns into an acknowledgement of her territory and rights. Connections are made between us that have little to do with reason: she somehow knows, in the immediacy of her perceptions and in the enigmatic depths of her experience, exactly what this confrontation is about, its essence; and I know, though I cannot explain or justify it, that she knows. The shudder that runs through me now is no longer my fright. It is the delight of animal recognition.

The scene is domestic: a man with short-cropped grey hair kneels on the hearth of a brick fireplace brushing a female dog of mixed origin. Fairly large and with a pelt of light brown and white overlaid with a pattern in black, the mongrel appears to have some German Shepherd in her ancestry. She stands near and parallel to the picture plane, paws on the hardwood floor and the wooden trim of the hearth, in a state of calm acquiescence; her head is turned towards the viewer, and her eyes gaze outward from her interior world in blank, soulful rapture. Some strange shadow of sadness shades her brow, some subtle pain glimmers deep in her bliss, as if standing there in the man's embrace and submitting to his care were the re-enactment of the ancient and almost forgotten compromise of the canine beast with humankind. The man, dressed darkly in casual clothes and compressed in the shallow space between the dog and the red brick fireplace, hunches from his knees over the dog's back, face intently absorbed. His eyes are not focussed, it would seem, on what he is doing, though his posture belies meticulous care. His left arm is bent around the dog's neck, and his left hand, fingers spread, gently holds her upper chest. His right hand holds a brush on her back, above her hindquarters. As if he were pushed upward and forward by the compression of the space in which he crouches, the man hovers protectively over the dog, his gesture of solicitous, loving appropriation resuming the ambiguous history of domestication. In the near middle ground, with its hearth advancing into the foreground, the unlit fireplace stacked with wood consolidates the physical closeness of the dog and her groom in the manner of a frame, placing their problematic relationship on display. The white mantlepiece is exactly in line with the crown of the man's head. There is no background to this picture, only the opaque surface of the bricks and walls which define the enclosed space of human habitation.

The rectangular format of this highly centred picture can be understood as the product of an equilateral triangle with its base coinciding with the bottom framing edge of the painting. This serves to group the dog and her groom in tight proximity and to focus attention on their relationship. If a circle constructed with a diameter equal to the height of the triangle is centred within the rectangle, as its arc descends on the left, it touches on the dog's right hind foot and, proceeding upward, passes by the man's visible foot, neatly enclosing the two protagonists. In this space, the roundness of the man's head is likened to that of the dog, and the arching, semi-circular sweep of his back is complemented by the graceful, downward curves of the dog's back, hindquarters and tail. If a hexagon is inscribed within the circle, its base corresponds to the bottom of the dog's feet closest to the viewer, and its top, to the line between the moulding and front board of the mantle, serving to further compress the space occupied by dog and man. The sides of the equilateral triangle

This is a kind of parody of the great Stubbs paintings of horses. The dog Min was, in a way, sent to us; she is classified at the veterinary clinic as "Shepherd X".

Alex Colville, "Remarks", November 1993

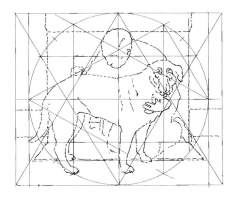

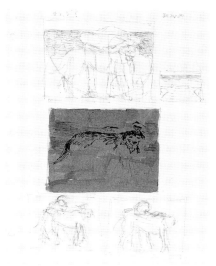

13.01

whose base is congruent with the bottom of the picture run through the dog's snout and hindquarters, and its apex tightly frames the man's head high in the centre of the picture, just above the central vanishing point, which corresponds to the position of the groom's eyes. From this rigorously structured space, the dog gazes outward into the everyday world of the viewer.

The dog and her groom know each other well, so well that it is difficult for us to break into the habits of their intimacy. She is at home with him, and they, together, united by the symbiotic bonds of domestication, are at home on the hearth. This is their place. His care is so long practised, so finely attuned to her manner, that he need not watch himself work; he holds, he brushes, he feels the tone of her presence, and his mind can safely dwell elsewhere. Our only access to this relationship is though the dog's humid gaze; there, behind the gleam, is an unfathomable space filled with incomprehensible depths of deep amber. Subtle thoughts and sudden memories flicker and diffract in the warm liquid glow, hopes and pains, too. Not our thoughts though, or our memories; not our hopes, or our pains. What the movements of her mind might be escapes us, their maverick shapes elude our grasp. Centuries of breeding and training have so inscribed human will and desire into domesticated animals that what we think we recognize as their being is only our reflection. But this dog is different. In her body as in the depths of her mind, she ultimately resists the pressure of human will. She does not conform to good breeding standards. She breaks the rules. She is touched by the wild. She is just a mutt, a mongrel. Could this be why he loves her so?

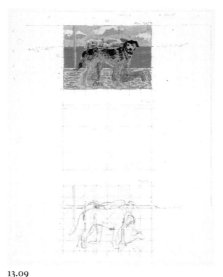

13.09

13. DOG AND GROOM, 1991

Acrylic polymer emulsion on Masonite
62.4 x 72 cm
Private collection

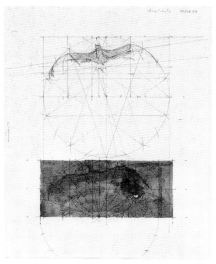

14.04

The blue sky glow of late evening has begun to sink under the hushed velvet of this summer night, silhouetting, as we look up from the street to the right, the rounded crowns of trees still attempting to display their green in the shadowed light. A bit farther away, a pole and the peak of a roof appear; closer, another pole stands vertical, stark against the trees and the sky, holding the illuminated half-globe of a street lamp on the end of a metal rod which rises at an angle above the invisible sidewalk. A soft ring of light radiates from the lamp, reflecting on the rod and pole. The tranquillity of the moment is broken for just one instant by the barely audible whisper of wings as a bat swoops overhead, veering slightly to the left, darker yet than the darkening evening sky. It flies as lightly as a breeze, this oval body of satin brown fur, its mouth open, crying out the inaudible sonar which guides its course, its ears erect to capture echoes. It stalls for the instant of our glance, this mysterious animal, on the delicate, silky membrane stretched between its fingers. On the leading edge of each extended wing, the concave sweep of the upper arm and ulna stretching to the thumb is followed by the convex curve of the second metacarpal; on the back edge, the rhythmic scalloping of the line moves from finger to finger, on to the tibia, and then ends in the point of the triangulated tail. The bat swoops overhead in the hushed velvet of this summer night. We can barely feel the whisper of its wondrous wings.

Scaled to present the bat life-size, this painting is quite small; its format, a root-5 rectangle, has been used to centre attention on the tilting sweep of the animal's flight. The rectangle can be subdivided into two contiguous squares and an additional rectangle on the right side formed by dropping an arc with a radius the length of the diagonal of the contiguous squares to an extension of their base line. The two squares are subdivided according to the rules of Le Corbusier's Modulor, and a semicircle is inscribed from the right to left bottom corners of the squares using as centre the point where they meet on the base line. The semicircle is then divided into ten equal segments. In the painting, these divisions regulate the positions of key elements and relationships. The left edge of the lamppost runs along the line between the squares and the additional rectangle to the right; the lamplight and the imprecise massing of the left edge of the trees, as well as the bat's left foot, all line up with rhythmic divisions of the Modulor. The bat's left ear is located just below the place of the right angle in the Modulor. The bat's wings fit neatly into the top of the semicircle; its tilt, about 9 degrees from horizontal, follows lines joining opposite, uneven segment points of the semicircle, the upper point always being in the right quarter. The axis of the bat's body is on the line that runs from the centre point of the semicircle to intersect the tilt lines at right angles. The viewer is standing on the street, in line with the median of the whole root-5 rectangle and below the lower framing edge of the picture.

14. BAT, 1989

Acrylic polymer emulsion on Masonite

12.6 x 28.2 cm

J. Rosenthal collection

The bat hears us standing silent in the street; it sheers up to the left, our presence echoing in its mind. What is it we feel in this so fleeting glimpse, what emotions are stirred in our souls? Is this the sentiment of awe, that mysterious sense of admiration tinged with the sudden respect of a caught breath? Is it the warm illumination of that grace which descends upon us so unexpectedly when we discover beauty? Perhaps, but is there not a vague, repressed shudder as well? Something is getting in the way, something troubled and sinister, something that clutches at our expanding hearts to constrain the impulse of wonder. We shiver now with a nameless fear, as if the bat's dark wings had enveloped us in the indistinct terror of night. Whence arises this blind closure of our admiration? No reasons explain this dread, no arguments dispel the panic. How can we think that this most accomplished of fliers, capable of avoiding a single hair in its flight path, will inadvertently get tangled in our well-groomed manes? The fear is groundless, but perpetuated just the same. The bat is a victim, not just of your and my irrationality, but of the stories told in our culture that impute evil, that malign, that pervert our recognition of the truth. The stories instruct us how to feel, reject and destroy at the very moment when simple wonder could move us to care. The bat, like the other wild beasts that still manage to remain, veers out of our way. It, with reason, is afraid of us.

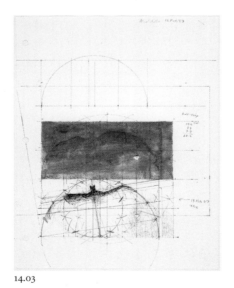

14.03

A black piano stands, lid raised at an angle bisecting the whole picture plane, in front of a triple sash window trimmed in white. The open drapes fall in gathered folds at each side of the window, more visible on the left than on the right. It is dark outside, heightening the windowpanes' reflectivity. Together, the window and the drapes form the middle ground of the picture and turn the compressed foreground back upon itself. From behind the piano, where the viewer is standing, the head of a young woman, partly obscured by the instrument, can be seen in the shallow space between the keys and the window. Her reflection on the glass, showing her from the back, brown hair spilling down to her shoulders, confirms that she is at the keyboard. Her dress is red. An intense light shines on her from the right, highlighting the full, young features of her face and contrasting them with the stark, hard lines of the piano and the dark of night beyond. Nothing else in the room can be seen in the sheen of light on the window. In this absence, the woman's head is thrown back at a slight angle in ecstatic joy, her visible eye is closed, and her mouth is open in joyous song.

The rectangular format in the proportion of 2 to 3 lends itself to subdivision into a grid and is used here in conjunction with asymmetry to suggest the release of sound in song. When the rectangle is divided vertically into three equal segments, the lines fall along the inner edges of the centre windowpane, creating a strong, balanced horizontal distribution of frames. If a square with sides equal to the height of the rectangle is centred in the picture and subdivided by diagonals from corner to corner, when a circle is inscribed within this square, the points where the diagonals and the circle intersect correspond to the top edge of the piano case and the line formed by the tops of the lower windowpanes. The distance from these lines to the bottom and top framing edges is equal, and it is repeated in the width of the curtain to the left, producing a slight asymmetrical weight on that side of the picture. When the whole is divided into quadrants, it becomes apparent that the young woman's head is located immediately below and to the left of centre and that her reflection is also displaced to the left of the centre windowpane. Two angles break away from the grid and play in counterpoint with the left-leaning asymmetry of the image: the raised piano lid, and the woman's head tilted slightly against the leftward lean of her body and thrown back in the song she sings.

With only our eyes to hear, what can we tell of this song? Of what shape, what colour is it? Do you see the full ease of the extended throat? There is none of the constriction, none of the tightness of the thin, pointed vowels; absent are the silver, darting sparkle that closes off an "i" and the compact steely shudder of an "e". The shape of the mouth, too, lets us hear; it sounds neither the inquisitive, high and

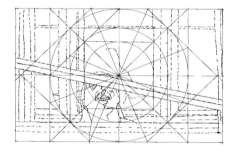

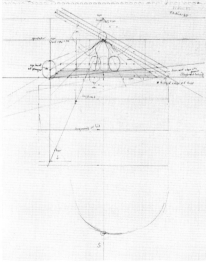

15.03

rounded "hooo" of the night owl nor the grave, urgent "ooo" of the Mourning Dove. Nor is it the perfectly circular "o" of surprise displayed on those lips. What we see is the golden oval of "ah" issuing enthusiastically from the throat, resonating through the chambers of the mouth and mind, floating, swelling, flowing outward to flood the room with the freedom of sunlight. The first vowel, the first letter, it announces not the beginning of pain as with the infant's first cry, but a total and overwhelming congruence with the origin of joy in the simple choice to live. The ecstatic fullness of being wells up within: "ah" is the song that sings the singer.

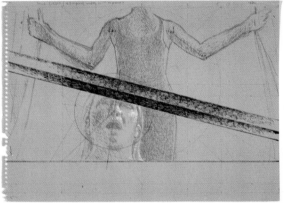

15.07

15. SINGER, 1986

Acrylic polymer emulsion on Masonite
40 x 60 cm
Galerie Claude Bernard, Paris

There is often a very close connection between girls and horses – very different from the relationship between Count Vronsky and his horse in the prophetic race in "Anna Karenina". In my painting the girl and the horse are doing something dangerous and exciting – crazy but necessary.

Alex Colville, "Remarks", November 1993

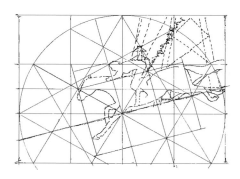

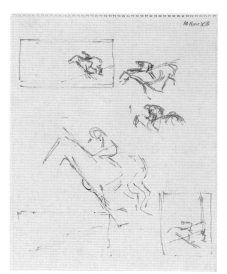

16.01

A dapple-grey thoroughbred flies down the brownish grey-and-yellow-spangled slope of a hill, its profile outlined against a dense forest of highlighted evergreens and a mottled, cloud-filled sky. None of the horse's hooves touch the ground as it rockets down the incline from right to left, carrying its rider high in her stirrups and raised from the saddle, body aligned with the animal's trajectory. She wears black riding boots and light beige pants, a sweater of rich violet, safety goggles and a geometrically patterned brown cap, visor turned to the back over her light brown hair. She is properly equipped. She knows what she is doing. She has the horse's energy controlled by her collaborative posture and her grip on the reins. Behind her, running parallel to the triangular forest's edge, is an equally triangulated pattern of hydro pylons and wires which disappear from view behind the horse. The invisible, impersonal power which they carry encounters the manifest animal power of the horse at the picture's vanishing point.

The format of *Horse and Girl* is a rectangle in proportions of 3 to 4; it is used to locate the horse in a square – the animal's length measured from nostrils to the most extended hoof equals the height of the painting – and to direct the implicit plunge of horse and rider from the right towards the vacant area of landscape produced by extending the square one proportional unit to the left. The impression of speed given by the horse's outstretched neck and head, its flying hooves and tail, and the girl's deep lean to the front is greatly enhanced by the division of the surface into related triangles. If a circle is drawn to fit comfortably within the picture by placing a compass on the vanishing point that lies on the vertical median, high on the horse's left front leg, it becomes apparent that the hydro wires, the tips of the evergreens, the sloping edge of the hill and the horse's left leg all correspond to radii of the circle. Contrasting with the wires which rise up and out from the centre, the edge of the hill runs across and downward, reinforcing the precipitous descent of the horse and girl.

The girl is totally absorbed in the ride; she crouches over the horses's mane, lining up the axis of her body with that of her steed and adjusting her balance with slight shifts of weight on the stirrups. Her every movement, each slight command from her hands, is felt by the horse, and she feels its response. They are in this together, these two with wind streaming in their faces; with the care and discipline of the equestrian arts, they have become a united vital force plunging through space. Implicated as she is, the girl cannot notice what we, mere onlookers, can see: the coincidence, from this exact angle and at this exact moment, of her trajectory with that of the hydro lines. But for us to whom this purely visual crossing of powers has been revealed, what could appear as an arbitrary juxtaposition can also be grasped

16. HORSE AND GIRL, 1984

Acrylic polymer emulsion on Masonite
45 x 60 cm
Private collection

as the site of a deep and troubling conundrum. The powers contrasted here are the natural body and technological culture; the questions raised concern their relationship. Developments in technology are usually justified by the common sense of our culture as a way of liberating us from drudgery, particularly by extending the boundaries of our physical limitations. What in fact happens, however, is that as technology becomes an integral part of our daily landscape, it imposes its own requirements and goals. The promised liberation then becomes a new type of dependency, a new kind of enslavement. Herein lies the anguished doubt of our times: Can we harmonize the energies by which we attempt to inhabit the physical world as corporeal, participatory beings, with technological transformations that bear within themselves not only the goals we unthinkingly call "progress" but also a high potential for the destruction of our personal wholeness and integrity? A model of creative partnership, the girl and her horse are a warm sign of hope in a landscape where cold metallic hydro poles stand in feigned innocence, pretending that they are no different than trees.

16.06

The sky is overcast with a veil of blue-grey clouds, and a soft, diaphanous glow of filtered sunlight cloaks the olive green and deep yellow expanse of a crop ripening in the lowlands. In the distance, far beyond a dike which runs across the picture behind the open field, the horizon is marked by the intermittent appearance of lavender hilltops. A fence recedes obliquely from the lower left corner of the image along a dirt road into the midground where both disappear, hidden from sight by a stand of untended bushes growing in a row parallel to the picture plane. The space behind the screen of scraggly bushes is partially obscured but nevertheless perceptible; a diamond-shaped marker or sign, facing away from the viewer into the distance, stands at an angle not far beyond the bushes to the right of the picture, indicating something that remains irremediably invisible. The fence and bushes frame an abandoned lot overgrown with billowing waves of mature grasses and, in the lower right foreground, a clump of wild roses in bloom. From amongst the grasses, supported by a three-tiered base and enclosed in the strong, rectilinear elements of a wrought iron fence, rises an ornate metal cross in profile against the solemn sky. On its upright, below the decorative iron motif which marks its intersection with the crossbeam, it bears an illegible memorial plaque in the form of a shield or a coat of arms. A woman with hair as dark and as strongly delineated as the cross and the plaque rides a horse bareback down the road into the foreground. She is wearing a sweater, lilac like the distant hills; the horse is chestnut. Both tints reverberate on the base of the cross. The horse moves forward at an easy walk and has already passed by the cross. Twisting her body from the waist and turning her head over her shoulder, the woman continues to fix her gaze on the dark emblem of Christian belief as the horse moves on.

The bearing of *French Cross* is focussed in the mediation of the viewer's relationship with the cross through the woman's absorbed look. Because the format of the work, a root-2 rectangle, can be produced either to the right or the left of the original square, two implicit vertical divisions of the subsequent rectangle can be envisioned. The placement of the cross and the rider and consequently their spacing have been determined in this manner: the right side of the cross coincides with the right side of the square if the square is placed in the left side of the rectangle; the central axis of the woman's head and body, and the horse's left shoulder and leg correspond to the left side of the square when placed in the right side of the rectangle. The distance between the woman and the cross, the space traversed by her gaze, occupies the central area of the painting and is framed by two equal spaces on either side. A balanced asymmetry activates the look and its mediating role. If the painting is divided horizontally through the centre, the strong, stable form of the cross at the top right counterbalances the mass of the horse and the woman to the lower left;

This cross, which marks the spot from which the Acadians were expelled in 1755, has interested me for a long time. I found a way of incorporating it when I thought of a girl, the daughter of a Chinese professor of mathematics, riding her horse past it. As far as I know, this never happened.

Alex Colville, "Remarks", November 1993

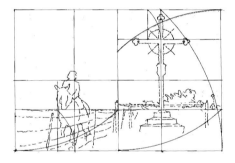

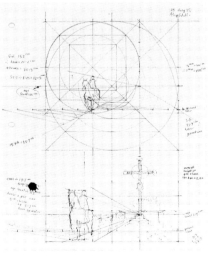

17.07

the woman's turned head rises starkly above the division line against the open grey cloud cover which contrasts with the dense grassy yard in the lower right. The viewer is off centre, located in the yard in line with the cross and at the height of the top of its base, separated from it by the wrought iron enclosure and from the woman and horse by the wire fence. The horizon line joins the top of the base and the mass of the horse, completing a triangularity of regards.

The cross becomes the protagonist as the viewer's usual concerns are displaced for the while by the woman's rapt attention. In a moment, when the horse moves on, her gaze will be torn away. And for each of us standing here in the unruly grass, our involvement is no doubt less a question of knowledge than of belief. Some of us dwell in the certitude of Christian faith; some did, but no longer do. Some believe other things about God; some, nothing at all. Despite our backgrounds and belief systems, we meet at the cross, which stands – though used and misused – as a sign, a symbol that has played its part in shaping the culture we share. We know the history, and, identifying in our own ways with the woman's gaze, we recognize our differences. But the *shape* is there for all of us; the immanence of the horizontal, our being here, and the transcendence of the vertical, our life purpose, meet, and their junction marks a critical point, a place for a pause, for reflection, for questions about choices to be made. *French Cross* is pregnant with possibility. At our feet blooms the wild rose, fragrant, its hooked thorns hidden in the foliage.

head turned more
27 July 82

17.09

17. FRENCH CROSS, 1988

Acrylic polymer emulsion on Masonite
56.5 x 80 cm
Garth H. Drabinsky collection, Toronto

The Chaplain, wearing the black cassock with stiff white collar and plastron appropriate for officiating at Divine Office, is seated in meditation in the chair behind the pulpit. The church is still, absolutely silent, as if nobody were present to disturb with their shadows the stark perfection of the white walls and woodwork or to sound their footsteps on the cold gleaming of the grey stone floor. You are there though, invisible as you sit in the front pew, waiting, watching, observing the desolate immobility of the Chaplain through the spindles of the pulpit. He is facing sideways, across the church, and notices nothing in his self-absorption. Your eyes have caught him unawares, and you feel uncomfortable, as if you were a voyeur. Though you cannot see his eyes, his demeanour suggests much. In his pursed lips and the set of his jowl are written the stoic firmness of those beset with inner struggle. His hands speak too, of deliberate acceptance, of weary resignation. What this anguish is, could be, is his secret. Whatever it might be – a sudden crisis of solitude, of despair perhaps, a state of mind arising from some recent occurrence, or a well-charted, dark desert of the spirit in which he has long wandered and now finds his home – he has not given up. He keeps a grip on himself by doing little things: the hair he still claims on his bald head is well trimmed, and his shoes are the image of perfect care. It comes to mind that the spindles of the pulpit are like the bars of a cage, a prison cell, locking the Chaplain in solitary confinement.

The combination of a rectangular format generated from geometric figures embedded in a square and two-point perspective contributes a great deal to the feeling of isolation and confinement produced by this picture. A square with the same height as the picture is located so that its right side corresponds to the right framing edge, which places the square's left side in line with the Chaplain's foot and the protruding edge of the boxlike architectural detail in the corner of the church. A circle is inscribed so that it meets the midpoints of this square's sides, and an octagon is inscribed inside the square and outside the circle so that the midpoints of the octagon's sides touch the circle. The oblique left sides of the octagon are continued in their respective slopes until they meet on the extended horizontal median of the square. A second square is inscribed within the circle; its left edge corresponds to the first spindle at the bottom of the pulpit's stairs. A measure equal to the width of the band between the first and second squares is added to the horizontal median from the point already determined by the octagon's sides. A vertical line can then be drawn to join the extended top and bottom of the first square and produce the left side of a rectangle, thus completing the format of the picture. The embedding of geometric shapes and proportions can be continued, setting an equilateral diamond within the first square by joining the latter's midpoints. Then a circle is inscribed within the diamond and, using the horizontal and vertical medians to form quadrants, subdivided

18. CHAPLAIN, 1991

Acrylic polymer emulsion on Masonite
68 x 92 cm
Private collection

by radii diverging at 22.5 degrees. The radii are extended to meet the framing edge on three sides and to two points where they meet extensions of the sides of the diamond on the left-hand framing edge. In relation to this pattern of embedded forms, the architectural elements of the church are laid out in two-point perspective so that the recession of the pulpit cages the Chaplain in a narrow, compressed space. The Chaplain's hands are held where the horizontal and vertical medians of the rectangle cross. The angle of the top edge of the rise in the stairs' trim corresponds to a diagonal of the original square, neatly tying the image and its format together.

Is this perhaps the image of a messenger who has lost the message? The story certainly began with his deep convictions, his adherence to the faith, his strong belief in his vocation. Because of his mission, he willingly dressed himself in the habit of the Church and stepped into the pulpit; he became a man of the cloth, and people, recognizing him by his uniform, called him "Chaplain". But as his title became his name, it also separated him from those he served, just as the pulpit stands apart from the pews. Awkward and isolating, this distance. But a necessary part of daily life. What feelings of care and consolation he had would have come from his reliance on the message he so passionately carried to his flock. All this no doubt worked well as long as his belief held him steady in its clear, explanatory light. There was purpose in his daily renewed exercise of charity, in his stringent self-discipline. But what if what we see now in his face is the dark, paralyzing pain of deep incertitude? Then he no longer has his confidence, no more his purpose; he has no more feeling at all. Could his doubt have started as he was quite innocently exercising his mind, developing arguments, answering objections, but this time, instead of staying out in the mental space reserved for thinking, the methodical questions turned around and struck directly at the place where his heart and his belly meet, struck, hitting hard, with the thudding impact of lead? First, the insidious, tentacled shadows of doubt would have spread outward, feeding on his confusion and fear, deepening to numb his mind and fingertips in an ever-denser obscurity. Then, to the very centre of his being the deadly shades would plunge, glowing with the fascination of onyx and obsidian. In these nether regions of impalpable darkness, in this silent vortex of weary emptiness, what might have been, what could have been, what never, never shall be, beckons now, calling out to the Chaplain as it could to any of us, entreating, seducing, promising peace with the implosion of the soul. Located somehow outside of himself, the Chaplain would then gaze inward to the lightless gulf, into this hole in his being, feeling its gravitational pull and knowing this to be the most awful temptation of all. The allure of nothingness. His faith, when shrouded in the night of his soul, is of no avail. With nothing left to give, there remains for him only the difficult task of hope. He sits, then, and waits for the light to return.

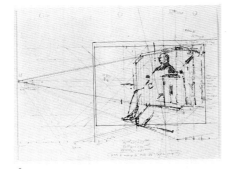

18.03

The scene of the action is a truck stop. A blond woman in a fur coat and violet slacks stands angled to the right, her back to the viewer, facing a man in dark brown coveralls and plaid cap. In the blue-grey gloom, the massive front wheel and red cab of a truck juts from the left almost into the line of sight between the woman and the man, its chrome radiator and bumper strongly illuminated, like the couple, by a bright light shining horizontally into the scene from the right, a shimmering halogen white with the silver shivers of early morning or the icy glitter of a chill late autumn evening. Above the cab, in the narrow space between the hood and the painting's top edge, leafless branches are silhouetted against an area of sky shaded blue darker than day. Behind the head of the man another truck is parked, the trailer blocking a view into the distance with the gridded rectangle of its side. The action is closer to us. The man, standing on tiptoe, holds a camera to his eye with both hands, obscuring the features of his face. He is taking a picture of the woman. She appears self-conscious in the glare, left arm raised to her head but her hand invisible, right leg advanced in a somewhat awkward imitation of a model's pose. Above her head, the words "Western Star" identifying the red cab seem to be a caption intended for her image.

The square format of this picture lends itself to regular vertical subdivisions to which various components of the image correspond. The vertical median runs through the woman's advanced foot, the centre of the red cab's tire, through the woman's lower arm and elbow, between the words "Western" and "Star", then up the back edge of the trailer that blocks the view at the picture's middle ground. The line subdividing the left half of the picture into two vertical bands frames the woman on her shaded side and leaves the band at the extreme left to be occupied by mechanical elements of the truck. To the right of the median, there is another band featuring the truck, and then, to the right of the subdivision that corresponds to the bright vertical glare on the truck's radiator, stands the man with his camera. A band the width of the distance from the woman's foot to the bottom framing edge can be imagined running around the inside edge of the picture, creating a virtual square within the actual square of the format. This band approximates the man's distance from the right framing edge and the distance of the top of the truck's red hood to the top framing edge, setting the visible area of sky into the border. Considered in regard to the depth at which the various figures are located, this arrangement produces a layering: occupying three-quarters of the total width, the red cab establishes a strong middle foreground, pushing the woman, in her one-quarter of the width, out towards the picture plane and squeezing the man into his quarter of the middle ground. Combined with the oblique angle at which the woman and man face each other in the confined space of the picture, this use of regular, stable subdivisions to

The woman has briefly become a model, the coveralled man has become an artist, fascinated by her. She, like the truck, is a "Western Star" – which is an actual make of truck. Painted after spending two months in the Orient.

Alex Colville, "Remarks", November 1993

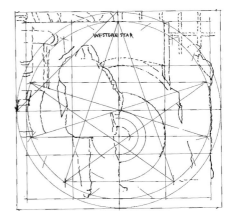

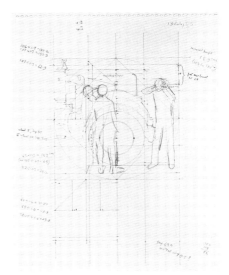

19.04

19.06

position the figures in an asymmetrical pattern tends to accentuate the couple's bilateral relationship while setting up the red truck as an intruder or at least the potential agent of separation.

On the days I have to teach early classes, I like to have breakfast at the Clearview Restaurant, on the edge of town. When I pull into the stop, I try to park my half-ton over to the side, out of the way of the big rigs. Maybe it's because they make my truck feel puny, with its light loads and short hauls, but I tell myself that I get a better view from here, just a bit above ordinary eye level, and Katie over in the diner can see me drive in and place my order while I just sit taking it all in for a while. By the way, she's a really good waitress and you can tell she knows what the place is about. She smiles as the drivers come in, calls them by their first names. When she brings the coffee she chats a bit and you can see she doesn't pry and gives everyone a chance to feel at home. There's a lot of talking then. Everyone is from somewhere, going somewhere. They've all left so much behind and hope to find so much when they get wherever they think they are going; they stop here just long enough to catch a breath and break the monotony of being alone on the road. And you know, the stop isn't really somewhere you'd want to live or go for a holiday – it's more of an intersection where solitary people meet, recognize their loneliness without actually admitting it, then go on their way encouraged by the unassuming gentleness of smiles and a bit of conversation. That's the sort of thing going on in the lot right now. The man almost steps forward in his eagerness to try and capture some moments of joy in the memory of an image; she hesitates to respond, knowing that what was precious in those moments is already past. But she complies, though with a touch of awkwardness, because the tenderness still exists. Who is she, this woman starring as Venus in the glare of headlights? A hitchhiker or a long-haul companion? Right now, that's not what's important. See, in his urgent gesture, can you see what she really is? His refulgent evening star, flashing iridescent waves of joy over the eternal moon. His morning star, glowing as he wakes to another, more tender dawn.

19. WESTERN STAR, 1985

Acrylic polymer emulsion on Masonite
73.8 x 73.8 cm
Musée d'art contemporain de Montréal, Lavalin Collection

The taxi is on the point of descending the steep incline of a street which falls away invisible under the windshield towards a port below. Through the windshield and side window, an angled bank of light grey and yellow highrises fills the central and right side of the view with an apartment terrace, stacked porches and windows, and a sign saying "Winston". Framed by the buildings and the head of a woman in the left front seat and partly obscured by the taxi's rearview mirror, appear pale blue waters reflecting an equally pale yellow form, perhaps a cloud bank above. Four large ships sail by. The driver, seen from the left back seat, is on the right side behind the steering wheel, driving in the English manner. His jet black hair and the outline of his high cheekbone and the facial contours of the woman seated to his left suggest that they are Asian. The driver's forehead, the left side of his head and the tip of his left ear can be seen in the rearview mirror. Jutting from the sun visor in front of the driver is a white sheet of paper or carton inscribed in red with Chinese ideograms; a piece of paper has likewise been tucked behind the visor in front of the woman, but no legible print appears on it. The taxi is at work; the for-hire sign is down and the meter reads "5.00". In the left bottom corner of the picture, in the immediate foreground, a hand holds the map of a port city, as if the viewer were verifying the taxi's location or route. From what can be seen in and from this taxi, the viewer is most likely touring Hong Kong.

The format of *Taxi* is a rectangle in proportions of 2 to 3, a shape which lends itself to a vertical division into three or six equal segments. Here, this division is exploited in conjunction with a high vanishing point strongly decentred to the left, which accentuates the impression of impending, vertiginous descent towards the harbour below. Using a division into three segments and beginning at the right side of the painting, the first vertical line runs down the left side of the driver's face, intersects his shoulder near the point where the edge of his vest descends out of sight to the front, and encounters the second seam of the front seat upholstery. The next line drops along the far edge of the highrises, dividing them from the sea beyond, and, after passing through the fourth seam of the upholstery, runs down the left-hand crease in the map. Other key features are located on the lines dividing the image into vertical sixths. The visual weight of the image is located in its right lower two-thirds. If the medians are traced out, the vertical median runs down the far edge of the closest apartment building, and the horizontal runs through the driver's collar and cheek, the centre point of the picture, and the woman's cheek. In shape and position, the cab's meter and the rearview mirror echo each other and suggest the presence of an invisible, vertical plane parallel to the picture's surface against which the rising angled lines of the buildings play. These lead the eye to the less massive left segment of the image, where they meet below and slightly to the right of the

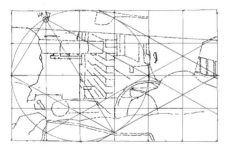

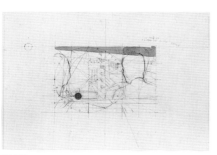

20.09

20. TAXI, 1985

Acrylic polymer emulsion on Masonite
40 x 60 cm
Private collection

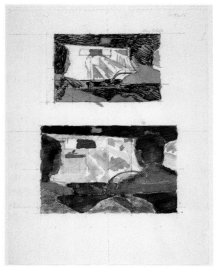

20.07

paper tucked behind the sun visor, high above the bay. For the eternity of a painted instant, the viewer is suspended on the cusp of the taxi's trajectory, floating above the sea and about to plunge.

I have never been to Hong Kong before, but this soaring instant nevertheless happens now in the framework of familiar memories. The feeling in the pit of your stomach is the same as when you gun the car just before the top of a steep overpass, except then you know what's going on. Have you ever been in Cape Breton? When you're driving towards Meat Cove on the road that hugs the cliffs, with the sea to one side and the rocky escarpment to the other, there is a place where a sudden turn is followed by a sharp drop that, for a moment of thrilling terror, leaves nothing to see but a vast azure expanse of water and sky. For a split second, gravity's tyranny relents, and you feel, fleetingly, the fear and ecstasy of flight. Then, as now, there is a mysterious harmony of spontaneous contrasts: the momentary, exhilarating suspension of weight, the uplifting leap of the gut, the instantaneous fear which strikes as the ordinary rules of the body are broken. And this can be a pleasure only if you know or intuitively trust that the road is still there, underneath it all. Trust in the continuity of things. Here, in Hong Kong, the taxi's lunge into the void is about the same feeling, but on a wider scale, as if it encapsulated what it's like to be a tourist. Being in a foreign place requires a suspension of habits, of easy confidence in things; so much is strange and disorienting when you travel. Here the traffic is on the wrong side of the street. The people speak a language you don't understand. Only the highrises are familiar. So having a map at hand helps you follow where you are going and keep some semblance of control. Nevertheless, without warning, the taxi leaps into space. There is a stab of terror. The driver and his companion are calm. In an instant the wheels will find the pavement once more.

Aimless and chill, the white diffused light of this overcast winter day penetrates the car's windshield and side window, spreading out in an even sheen over the sleek dark dashboard, highlighting my hands and the steering wheel they warmly grip. I am banking the car slightly to the left, doing almost seventy, to where the steel bridge crosses the frigid, leaden waters that cut across the snow-blanketed landscape. Here and there in the loosely packed accumulation, tire tracks cut through to the road below in parallel arcs; bushes marking the contours of the far shore shiver under grey frost. A hitchhiker in sombre winter garb stands alone on the right side of the road, mittened hands and stiff arms gesturing for a ride, fur hat turned towards the car. The rearview mirror obscures the hiker's face, replacing it with a glimpse through the back window at the bleak, frigid landscape left behind and a small portion of my forehead and greying temple. In the side mirror, the white expanse is reiterated. This moment, suspended between landscape past and landscape future, this possible encounter, is isolated, wrapped in the numbing solitude of a downcast winter day.

It seems to me that much of our experience of our surroundings is from the inside of a car, particularly if the car is a kind of pet, as this Porsche 911 is. The same bridge appears in the next few works.

Alex Colville, "Remarks", November 1993

The picture's format is constructed of two horizontally contiguous squares, and its scale is based on the actual size of the driver's hands. The semicircular shape of the steering wheel governs the layout of the image, positioning the viewer and drawing attention to the implied double movement of the car, forward and banking to the left. Centred on the vertical median, the top of the steering wheel falls somewhat short of the horizontal median and thereby fails to establish an equal division between the bottom and top halves of the image; seen in conjunction with the mass of the car, which also tends towards but does not quite reach the horizontal dividing line, this gap between the actual position of the car and the ideal position at the dividing line urges the car forward. This tendency towards the line of horizontal symmetry seems to be confirmed if an arc is inscribed using the same centre as the steering wheel but including the driver's knuckles: it rises just above the geometric centre of the image. The vanishing point is located about one-quarter of the distance from the centre to the top of the image, reinforcing the forward pull on the car. If another arc is inscribed using the centre of the steering wheel and the bottom corners of the picture, it rises through the bridge and descends through the hitchhiker's hat and the rearview mirror, establishing a connection between the two objects soliciting the driver's attention and choice.

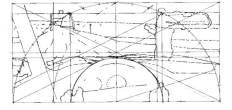

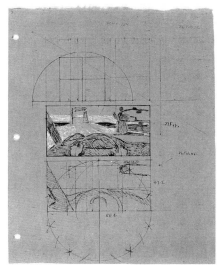

21.12

Why, today, does this simple choice seem so heavy to me? Maybe yesterday, with that bright sun and the faint perfumes of a slight thaw, I would have felt more expansive, more generous of heart – maybe yesterday I would have stopped, knowing full well it could change the course of my day. Or tomorrow maybe, tomorrow when I will feel more relaxed, with less on my mind. No, it's not that this choice is so different than any other, than any of those myriad bifurcations in life's path that question my personal agenda. Today what weighs so is the vast solitude, the isolating chill of this place, the shivering apprehension that envelopes my determination. I feel it in my hands – they grip the wheel, directing, controlling. Until now, I was secure in my purpose; on the road, going somewhere, my route set. And now, like a road sign, the hiker signals with semaphore arms, asking for a lift, calling perhaps for a change of plans. There is some danger in this moment, the double jeopardy of trust. Can I, in this desolate place, count on the hiker as a genuine fellow traveller? Even more, can I count on myself to deal with the unforeseen events, the newness, that this choice could provoke? Things do happen if you're open to their happening. Now, as the car banks towards the bridge, now, I must decide.

21. TRAVELLER, 1992

Acrylic polymer emulsion on Masonite
43.2 x 86.4 cm
Redpath Gallery, Vancouver

A car at night, tail lights, departure.
I even like Rodin's "The Kiss," and
Shakespeare's Antony:
"I am dying, Egypt, dying; only
I here importune death awhile, until
Of many thousand kisses the poor last
I lay upon thy lips."

Alex Colville, "Remarks", November 1993

To the top left of the picture, an amethystine sky glows with the light of dawn or of evening, barely illuminating a field which sweeps from behind the dark, silhouetted mass of trees in the picture's central and right middle ground, screening much of the view into the distance. A highway runs at an angle upward from the bottom right to the left side of the image, its white centre line broken. A white Honda is stopped in the middle of the right lane in front of the trees, its orange-red brake light burning, incandescent in the surrounding gloom, its front signal light gleaming intense yellow and the invisible headlights casting a swath of gold onto the road in front. A woman, dressed in a skirt and sweater of the same deep tones as the landscape, stands at the driver's door, one foot stepping on the highway's centre line, the other, behind, turned to the side and lifted at the heel. She leans forward, bending at the hips, one hand resting on the lower edge of the car's open window. From his position behind the steering wheel, the driver has leaned into the window opening, head thrown back. The driver and the woman are kissing. The viewer, located at a station point level with the horizon and to the extreme right of the picture, seems to have no clear reason for being present at this event, but he or she nevertheless is constituted as a witness to this intimate and enigmatic scene of departure.

The feeling of imminent departure suggested by the kiss is reinforced by a slight asymmetry in the placement of the man and woman, the contrast between the angles used in the surface pattern, and the decentred perspective. The horizontally rectangular format of the picture can be divided into two squares; these in turn can be subdivided both by a regular grid and by diagonals drawn from key points on the bottom and top framing edges. The car stands in the right-hand three-quarters of the image, leaving the illuminated road empty in the left quarter. The line at three-eights the width of the image from the left drops through the less dense branches of the trees in the middle ground to meet the woman's left thigh where it bends to form the angle of her back. The median runs through the back of her head, her shoulder and her elbow and, with the next grid line to the right, frames the kiss to the right of centre, provoking a slight asymmetry. This displacement to the right of centre works in conjunction with diagonals which slope parallel to the line formed by the woman's back and the car's radio antenna: the diagonal from the bottom left corner to the top median point runs through the bumper and the front signal light; the diagonal from the bottom centre of the left-hand square to the top centre of the right-hand square runs through the woman's left foot and right hand; and the line from the bottom centre point of the right-hand square to the outside centre point of the same square ties the centre of the back tire and the brake light. All these diagonals lean to the top right, away from the visual thrust of the decen-

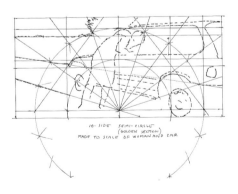

10-SIDE SEMI-CIRCLE
(GOLDEN SECTION)
MADE TO SCALE OF WOMAN AND CAR

0. KISS WITH HONDA, 1989

Acrylic polymer emulsion on Masonite
31 x 62 cm
[Location unknown]

tred two-point perspective which leads the eye at a less sharp angle towards the left. Strongly and clearly determined by the car's roof and dark trim and the road's white line and far edge, which cuts out of the picture at the point of the vertical golden section, the visual recession towards the left vanishing point, outside the picture, generates a feeling of potential movement. This directional flow is complemented by the repeated curves of the top corner of the rear window, the front of the car's roof, the woman's and man's heads, and the front fender. The movement is braked by the right-leaning diagonals and by the slight, momentary asymmetry of a farewell kiss.

They are trying to stop time, these two. He, leaning his head back and away from the future, welcomes her lips with his; she, bending into his uplifted face, turns her back on the impending moment. In the meeting of their lips the past rushes forward into the present, too urgently, too vibrantly, to adopt the shapes of fond memories. No, there is too much to contain in this kiss, the fondness of too many shared hours, the accumulated weight of joyful arrivals, the hurtful misunderstandings, the delights of an aimless day, the loving, the longing, too much to recall now. The meeting lips circumscribe the couple; the kiss seals them off for a suspended, but fleeting, instant in a shared, imageless world of awareness. They exist for each other. They realize, though, through the pulse, through the forgotten memory patterns of their bodies – they know – that presence always flees, chased by the anguish of an inexorable separateness of selves, the ultimate solitude. As if to resist what must be, to make it possible to grasp and hold this presence forever, they imagine an image of their kiss. But it brings distance, disrupting the tender, shared instant. Then, in the kiss, the dull pain of loneliness awakens. A prelude to departure.

The calm grey-blue surface of the sea recedes from the immediate foreground, to where, a quarter of the way up the picture, it glints turquoise and pale purple under the hazy satin mist of early morning. Glowing rose through the veils of the new day, the sun's warm disk floats in serene independence on the picture's horizontal median to the left of centre. No cloud formation floats as an island of security in the indeterminate depths of this sky, and no landmass interrupts the tranquil, immeasurable extension of this sea. But left of centre, close to the picture plane, a head emerges from the waters, disturbing the surface with a pattern of silent ripples. Monumental in scale, the head is covered in a white bathing cap which seems to be illuminated not by the warm spectrum of this sun's light, but by some other source, cooler and crystalline, above. The cap forms an oval which, as it descends around the swimmer's face, frames her eyes and the bridge of her nose before it disappears below the water. Her nostrils and mouth are submerged; no word or breath disturbs the immense, suspended silence of this liquid place and moment. Wide open and exactly level with the horizon line, the swimmer's eyes, haunted by some deep sorrow, look directly forward to the place in front of the picture where they meet our gaze.

The format of *Swimmer and Sun* is based on two and a half equilateral triangles aligned horizontally, the half unit located at the end of the sequence. When the format is completed by enclosing the triangles in a rectangle, a second sequence of inverted triangles appears, mirroring the first. While serving to establish the relative positions of the swimmer and the sun, this double sequence animates the surface of the painting with complementary left-to-right and right-to-left rhythms comparable to the barely perceptible pulse of the sea. The surface can also be divided into four equal horizontal bands, of which the lower is occupied by the sea and the upper three by the sky. The swimmer's head is centred in the second complete upright triangle from the left; if a line is drawn from the centre of the base of this triangle to the upper left corner of the picture, it runs through the horizontal median at the position of the sun. The oval of the bathing cap is geometrically related to the position of the swimmer's eyes, focussing attention on their mute gaze: each pupil is the centre of a circle, the double pivots around which the oval curves. The ripples circling the woman's head on the receding surface of the sea are drawn in perspective from a low position, locating the vanishing point of the picture behind the bridge of the woman's nose, at midpoint between her eyes. The viewer can hardly avoid questioning what sorrow is harboured there.

Among the myriad sadnesses that can inhabit our souls, it seems to me that some are dry and others humid. Dry sadness comes upon us like the desert wind, desic-

A woman as a kind of submarine. I may owe a debt to the film "Das Boot".

Alex Colville, "Remarks", 12 May 1994

cating, fossilizing the spirit, immobilizing the self, as in the case of the *Chaplain,* in the barren wasteland of an ineluctable, inert despair. Renewal of our confidence in life must then await an impulsion of a new energy that we feel comes from somewhere outside our selves, that happens to us as a gift. Humid sadness rises in a flow of internal harmonies as a response of our whole self to the plight of the world around us; like the ebb and flow of even the calmest of seas, this sorrow does not undo us, but is rather an integral movement of our being as it recognizes and responds to the fragile limits of all that we know, as it faces the radical condition of finitude. Animated by hope, it is a strong sorrow, a sadness which can channel energy into decisive, creative action.

Look again now if you will at that quiet sea under the eternal sun. Gaze once again into the swimmer's gaze. Here are the eyes of the sea, haunted with a sense of our fragile destiny. Here are the dual givers of life, the nurturers, the images of our hope, but here also is the tragic knowledge that the vivifying waters are not inexhaustible. The whales know, the once-innumerable fish know, the inhabitants of polluted seabeds know, the swimmer knows. She will not give up, nor should we, for this sadness is of the creative kind. To be strong, it must know itself. And so, before we answer the swimmer's appeal, it would perhaps be good for us to allow the humidity of our own sorrow to well up in our eyes until a least a few salty tears drop into the salty sea.

22. SWIMMER AND SUN, 1993

Acrylic polymer emulsion on Masonite
20.8 x 60 cm
Shearman & Sterling, Toronto

The Drawings

Ranging from rapid graphic notations jotted down with the first glimmers of a visual idea to final, carefully worked out studies, preparatory drawings for all but two of the works on display are included here. Those for the paintings are in two separate galleries, arranged in groups according to the final versions' titles. Unlike the finished works, which were conceived and executed to stand on their own in an exchange with the viewer, the drawings are not thought of by the artist as complete in themselves, but only as steps in the process of forming and transforming a visual idea until it reaches the state of a matured visual conception, a construction in which there is an adequation between what he is seeking and the image in which it is embodied. Unless the drawings are signed, Colville does not even necessarily think of them as satisfactory individual documents; they derive their interest from their status as factual occurrences within the artist's working process.

One of the purposes of physically distancing the drawings from their respective paintings in hanging this exhibition was to underscore the difference of status between the two kinds of work. Another was to avoid the danger that, in showing the drawings in close proximity to the paintings, there might be the implication that each series of drawings would provide access to the corresponding painting's meaning. This assumption would be confusing and could lead to erroneous conclusions. Since the content of a painting arises in the interactive relationship between the spectator and the work, Colville's personal research is pertinent in this instance only to the degree to which his position is inscribed in the work as it stands in the spectator's view. What is relevant is that the painting introduces an open-ended situation which requires the viewer's input, and that it is in this relationship that the final responsibility for content lies. In a quite different manner, the drawings cumulatively form a record of the artist's search for meaning; in this sense, they are reflexive. Their import is in what they articulate of the artist's experience as a producer of images. Although there is a connection and some overlap between the two forms of expression because they both embody the artist's viewpoint, their respective meanings are nevertheless far from coextensive. What Colville's drawings provide, then, is a collection of documentary evidence on which to base an exploration of his use of imagination, memory, observation, rational construction and skill in the examination of everyday situations concerning experiences of human value.

The term "drawing" is being used here in an uncommonly wide sense to designate the various kinds of graphic activities in which Colville engages to determine the subject matter and structure of his finished works. Centred on the notion of *delineation,* these activities include notations from memory, life studies based on motifs or models, measured plans, geometric patterns, studio compositions, photographs, photocopied and faxed imagery with additional graphic detailing, and Mylar overlays. Colville draws with graphite pencil, various colours of ink and, more rarely, wax crayon, dating images either individually or by the section of the layout on the page or support. While he has a preference for handmade paper, he also employs commercially prepared drawing pads, card and machine-compatible paper. Very frequently, an image is reworked on different occasions, producing an overlay effect. When doing this, Colville uses different colours or media during each work session and dates each layer with the appropriate colour or medium. These layered images are of particular interest because they clearly show the process of modification and adjustment of the elements and relationships which determines the final work.

12.01

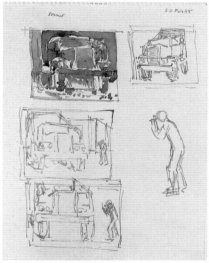

19.01

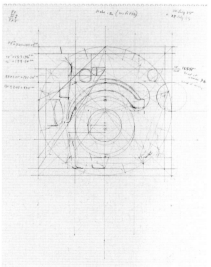

19.07

A cat crouches over a saucer. A naked woman stands in a bedroom with a revolver in her hand. A man holds a camera to his eye. At this point a mental representation germinates as a drawn form. Each grouping of Colville's drawings contains a sequence of key images – of people, things, situations – in various states of delineation and transformation. A dog joins the cat. The woman moves to the upstairs hall. The man goes to a truck stop.

Although it is difficult to determine with certitude a definite originating image for each painting, it is possible to identify the early stages of a working sequence because the drawings are then usually very tentative, loose and insubstantial. Composed of bare, wavering outlines or flowing, splotchy silhouettes, these images seem to be seeking their appropriate shapes, more often than not in raw sienna, sepia, maroon, yellow or orange ink, sometimes in combination with pencil. For the artist, black ink would usually be too definitive at this stage. As if they do not want to be alone, the figures seek appropriate companionship and placement in space. The subject matter becomes not so much the presentation of people and things, as of relationships. The dog hovers protectively over the cat. The woman towers over an ominous staircase. The man photographs to hold in memory a starlit moment of tenderness.

Colville's drawings record various aspects of his experience and relate to the final paintings in different ways. The things and places they depict are the things and places of his daily life, his home, town, region, of a place he has visited. The figures, however, neither too generalized nor totally individualized, belong to his mind. He draws untiringly, responding to the demands of the image in which he is currently involved or building up a stockpile of sketches to be used as the occasion demands. Some of these drawings never connect directly into a completed work, but fall into the background of his investigations, latent, awaiting activation. Whether the images he chooses to develop arise in his imagination as memories of things he holds close or whether they are notations from direct observation, whether they consist of isolated, vague impressions or set down the essence of some incident he has witnessed, they always function as markers of his interest in the possibilities of a subject area and open for him a roughly circumscribed field of investigation. Neither the final composition of a work nor its concrete import to the artist is completely given in the early key images; what they do access for us is his intuitive attachment to shadowy, indeterminate, originating figures which, centering his concern, express his first intuition of an unformulated meaning, his sense of undetermined potential, and his desire to work out implications.

Two rapid sketches done on 23 January 1988 show a side view of a figure lying face down on a boat, dangling an arm towards the water. One of the drawings, functioning as an inset, includes another figure standing behind the first. By mid-

February, while the side view is still being considered, the slightly angled frontal presentation finally used in *Looking Down* is also developed within a square format. A circle framing the boat and the two human figures, geometric patterns, perspective studies, measurements and annotations appear. The positions, dress and gestures of the couple are modified, the man's more than the woman's, for her position gazing into the sea remains fairly constant. On 8 and 9 March, a small drawing in acrylics shows the scene much as it appears in the painting, though some adjustments are yet to be made. An ink sketch dated 15 May delineates the contours of the far shore which appears on the horizon of *Looking Down*. Pencilled onto the same surface, in much larger scale, is a study in outline of the woman's head and face as seen from the top.

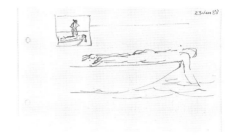

2.01

The development of a series can, when things come easily, take place over a few months but can also require a longer period of experimentation and maturation, sometimes several years. A direct sketch in maroon and black ink of a wrought iron cross in the countryside of Grand Pré, Nova Scotia, is dated 1983. Another, a diagrammatic drawing in dark brown ink annotated with the actual measurements of the cross and a remark about proportions, could be from the previous year. Since then at least, Colville wanted to feature the cross in a painting, but it was not until the summer of 1988 that the structure of the picture was finally resolved by using the young woman riding a horse found in *French Cross*. There is a hill in the region that inspires Colville with a sentiment of reverence. He would like to include it in a painting but has not yet been able to do so. It waits.

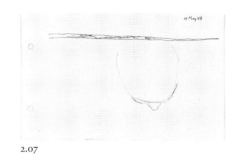

2.02

In the course of their development, Colville's key images change in various ways. The viewpoint adopted, the position, angle and scale of the main figures, the intervals or negative spaces between things, the whole scene or some of its aspects – any or all of these things are caught up in the process of transformation until a state of compositional stability occurs. Standing somewhat outside the flow of the key sequence, but generated or motivated by what is needed for its elaboration, are studies that serve several essential functions. The originating visual idea, to adopt an objective form, calls for a level of precision which will situate the final image between the generality of the early sketches and an overdetermined individualization or characterization of the subject matter. This level of precision, typical of Colville's work, produces the interpretative openness of his images. It involves three interdependent processes: *embodiment* of the subject matter through life drawings and diagrams using actual sites, objects and models or constructed maquettes or perhaps a combination of both; *geometric structuring* through the determination of format, the investigation of regulated surface divisions and the adoption of a system of perspective; and the *authentication* of the image to hold it in the sphere of likelihood by verifying its relationship to the world of everyday experience.

2.07

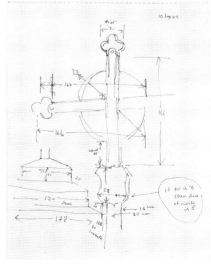

17.01

The selection of studies for *Low Tide* provides a good example of image transformation. The sketches from between 3 and 5 November 1986 show the boat, in most cases angled to the left out to sea, from a position on board. Two figures appear in the boat, one crouching on the foredeck near the railing, the other lying with bent knees raised in the foreground, feet to the left. The crouched figure, probably male, holds his hands up to his face as if using binoculars, and as the sketches progress, he changes his position from looking away into the distance towards the right to looking downward to the left as if examining something on the deck or immediately in front of the boat. The indicated eye level changes as well, corresponding in one case with the man's eyes, in others with a lower position. The other figure, which by 5 November is identifiably female, radically shifts position by moving her feet to the right side of the boat. In subsequent drawings, the exact position of her feet, flat on the deck or up on the railing, and the angle of her knees change. Always disposed parallel to the picture plane, she extends more or less across the width of the foreground. The man leaves the boat and stands in the tidal waters of the Minas Basin off the Bay of Fundy. Now he holds a mooring rope. Eye level merges with the depicted horizon line, and the vanishing point corresponds to the land formation known as Blomidon. A study of the woman made on 15 December shows that she has, in the interval, acquired a hat which she wears tilted over her face.

The rough sketches for *Couple on Bridge* dated 1 and 2 June 1992 introduce an excellent example of Colville's search for the precise gesture required by the originating idea. If the woman's position and posture – she leans one elbow on the railing, chin held in cupped hand – remain fairly constant, the man's change considerably. Always standing to the woman's left, his position moves slightly closer or farther as his body turns from an oblique front view to a side view and finally to an oblique back view, his arms first raised symmetrically up to shoulder and head height, hands flailing the air, then arranged asymmetrically, one hand held high, the other dropped by the railing in the direction of the woman. In the sequence of ink and Mylar images from 7 June, the position of the man seems to become fixed somewhere near arm's length from the woman, and he seems to stand at right angles or with back turned at a slight angle towards the viewer. His upper arms are now held more in to the sides, and his gesture towards the woman is based on a lift of the forearm from the elbow. By 3 and 4 July, the relative positions and gestures of the couple have been fixed and fleshed out satisfactorily enough for the artist to use a photocopy of the sketches of that date as the base for a colour study.

More often than not, Colville's wife Rhoda acts as the model for the female figures in his work, and he for the male. Rhoda posed for the *Floating Woman,* the woman who awaits the sailor's *Arrival,* and it is she who stands, a recalcitrant muse, beside the artist in *Couple on Bridge.* Usually Colville makes direct life drawings of

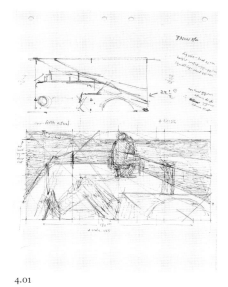

4.01

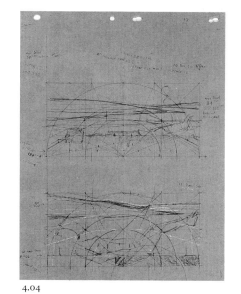

4.04

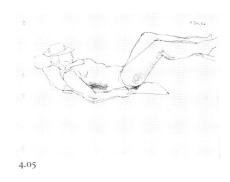

4.05

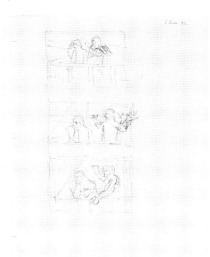

9.01

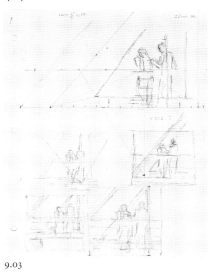

9.03

9.06

9.07

5   105 cms from
        picture plane
mirror out of focus

15.12

15.20

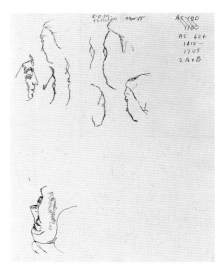

20.12

his models; sometimes, however, especially when the pose is exacting and difficult to hold, he uses photographs. For *Singer* he built a model of the piano and used it while staging some photographs; in the process, both he and Rhoda as well as the young woman who became the definitive model, posed for the camera, heads tilted. When appropriate, particular people are requested to model. The two men in *Target Shooting* are a neighbour and his son, the young woman photographed for *French Cross* is the daughter of a friend, and the model for *Chaplain* is a local minister, a friend of Colville's. There are at least two cases in which the model is another work of art: the woman's face in *Taxi* is based on sketches made on 4 April 1985 of a Chinese figure in the collection of the Royal Ontario Museum, while the human legs in *Cat and Dog,* and perhaps the positioning of the woman's legs in *Woman with Revolver,* are based on a Greek fragment in New York's Metropolitan Museum.

The domestic animals in *Cat and Dog* and *Dog and Groom* were modelled after pets of the Colvilles'. The *Bat,* however, is based on anatomical drawings and measurements derived from scientific illustrations. The extended, galloping movement of the horse and the forward crouched position of the rider in *Horse and Girl* were consolidated using a reversed copy of a news photograph captioned "Native Dancer Winning the Metropolitan".

Although the drawings for *Dog and Groom* consistently feature a dog standing parallel to the picture plane, head to the right side, and a figure kneeling behind the dog and brushing its fur, they show major shifts in the scene as a whole and exacting adjustments in the positions of the protagonists. Sketches dating from the end of September into December 1990 centre the action on a dock with the sea receding to a horizon situated at the level of the dog's back and eyes. The shoulders and head of the groom, apparently a man, lean strongly to the left; one hand is on the dog's rump, the other, outstretched to the right, holds the dog's neck. From sketch to sketch, the groom's position is adjusted to the left or right, with the head raised or lowered above the dog's rump, but usually tilted to look at an angle to the right. There is indecision about which hand holds the brush and whether the groom should be leaning on his right arm. On 7 January, the scene is still on a pier, but the groom has become a woman. She leans so low that her face is hidden behind the dog, her left arm bent above the dog's back in what seems to be a brushing motion to the left, and her weight is clearly supported by her right arm and hand. The dog seems to occupy somewhat less of the foreground. Later in January, the scene moves inside to locate the action in front of a fireplace. The groom is once more a man, for whom Colville acts as the model, but he crouches over the dog's shoulders and gazes downward to the left at the dog's back.

A series of drawings does not necessarily develop in a straight line from the early images to the final picture. There exist bifurcations, meanderings and encounters of

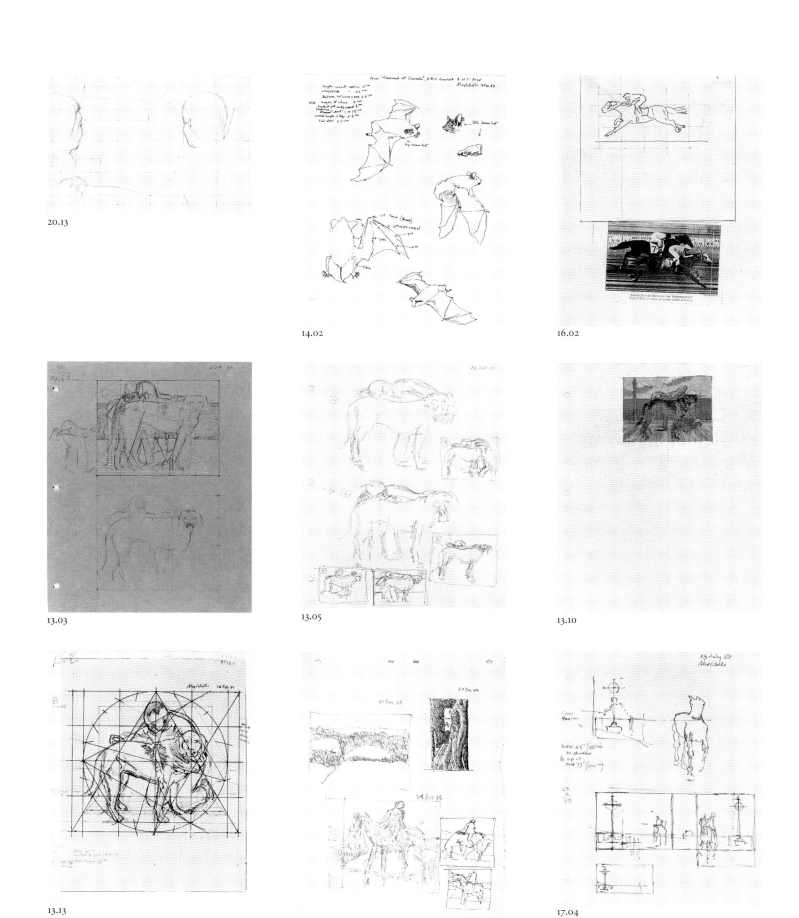

20.13

14.02

16.02

13.03

13.05

13.10

13.13

11.10

17.04

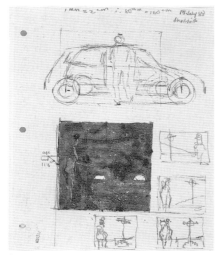

0.02

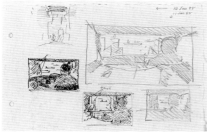

20.01

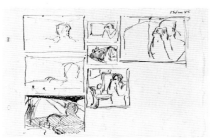

20.02

images which weave various series together and seem, in some instances, to imply an affinity of shapes. In late December 1986, Colville drew rapid sketches of a figure riding bareback on a horse; in some cases, the figure turns to look over her shoulder towards the right side of the image. The horse, whether walking, grazing or standing alert, is positioned almost parallel to the picture plane. There is at least one sketch from this period which shows the horse, head down to the ground, at right angles to the picture plane and at the extreme left of the image. These could be reminiscences of the earlier work *Horse and Girl,* but in July 1988, drawings in various formats and scales show Colville positioning and repositioning the horse and rider with the cross in *French Cross* and introducing the fence which mediates their relationship in the final work. In the same month, Colville was also doing studies for *Kiss with Honda.* On the 15th, a sketch of the car positioned parallel to the picture plane with a human figure at the front door, back to the viewer, and a dark wash drawing of the car facing frontward with a figure to the left at the door are accompanied by four small studies for *French Cross.* This juxtaposition of images in the intermediary stages of their development could merely indicate the artist's interest in several different situations; however, it may also indicate a deep thematic connection between them as well as a principle of formal differentiation. Both series deal with an at least potential directional movement in which the passage of one component of the portrayed action – the rider on the horse, the man in the car – is contrasted or opposed to the abiding presence of a component about to be left behind – the cross and the woman on the road. Similar also are the elements used in the linear construction of these works' pictorial spaces: the dirt road bordered by a fence, the highway with its broken white line and dark forested background; the angle of the horse and rider accentuating the recession of the dirt road, the angle of the car implying movement forward. Given these general similarities of theme and structure, each series of images, through implicit comparison, becomes a differential sequence which invests each final work with its own individuality, its own ability to generate the experience of singular content.

Similar to pages on which images are juxtaposed are those which seem to function as the generative matrix for works which, with time, become so highly differentiated through the process of pictorial construction that their commonality is obscured or even obliterated. In early 1985 Colville visited Hong Kong. On 11 January he made four sketches of a scene from inside a taxi using different sizes of horizontal rectangles. One of these images has the word "taxi" written above it, and all four are easily recognizable as forebears of the painting with that name. Of particular interest is the presence on the same page of a rapid sketch of a plunging street scene with two people climbing uphill, apparently a view of what would be seen if one were standing outside the taxi or sitting close to the window. But this image is dated the 10th, the day before the "taxi" sketches, suggesting that the view subsequently chosen from within the taxi was intended to emphasize the sudden drop to the harbour and that this involved editing out the street material as extraneous. Other things outside the taxi nevertheless remained of interest to the artist. On 13 January, along with three sketchy variants of the taxi theme, there are four images of what seems to be a male figure holding a camera to his eye. In three cases, a boat appears behind the man, each time at a different angle. In the fourth, the boat has been transformed into the outlines of a large truck. On 16 January, three sketches on one page continue the themes: one relates to *Taxi*; the second shows three figures, two seated and one standing, apparently on a dock where a large boat is moored; and the third picks up on the man-with-a-camera idea, suggesting his location on the dock and setting the boat farther in the background. On 23 January, two variants for *Taxi* appear along with an image of a bespectacled personage looking straight out from in front of the outline of a boat. The figure's forehead is positioned so that it separates the letters "HM EX" and "ESS", which appear in the middle ground. During this and the following year, three works related to these drawings were completed: *Taxi, Western Star* and the serigraph *Köln Express*. Of these, *Taxi* carries distinguishable signs of Hong Kong as its site of origin. *Western Star* has a North American flavour, and the *Köln Express* could be coming through almost any port in the world.

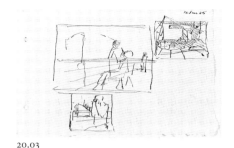

20.03

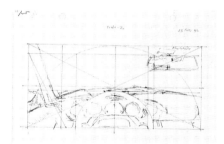

20.05

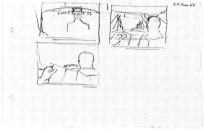

21.13

Geometric structuring involves the mutually dependent activities of format determination and surface regulation or patterning. For each possible format a corresponding set of appropriate surface patterns can be generated; conversely, surface patterns, depending on their use, call for an appropriate format. In Colville's work, neither format nor surface regulation is imposed on the subject matter; they grow out of the work's investigation of meaning.

As the components of an image are brought together and positioned in tentative arrangements, the picture soon calls for an appropriate and effective format. With some works, notably *Taxi* and *Traveller,* the format seems to be derived directly from visual constraints imposed by the viewer's position in the scene. In both of these pictures, the viewer's field of vision is marked out by the windshields of the vehicles, and these are in turn echoed by the framing edges. The derivation of the format is usually more complex, however, and seems to involve a generative principle. As shapes and relationships are established and transformed, the format responds, accommodating and enhancing the changes. This process is clearly illustrated in the drawings for *Singer.* During early November 1985, Colville made sketches of a player hunched over the keyboard of an upright piano viewed from the side, with a singer standing behind the instrument in the middle ground, mouth open in song. The format was a vertical rectangle. A little later, the piano player was inscribed within a circle, and with this potential isolation from the standing figure,

15.02

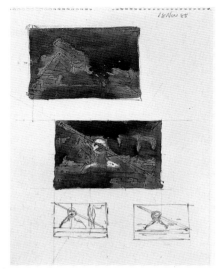

15.01

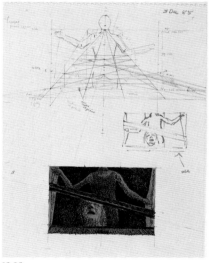

15.05

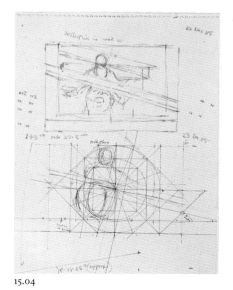

15.04

there was at least a suggestion of a circular format. Several pages of drawings dated the 18th of that month show variants of the scene. Some of these sketches include the two figures, the singer standing to the left of the player who crouches over the keys to the right; in these cases the format used is a vertical rectangle. In others, there is a conflation of the singer and the player into one figure seated at the keyboard, and the view is from the back of the piano. The format is then a horizontal rectangle. By 3 December, a page of sketches includes an image of the player-singer framed in a horizontal rectangle and bisected by the piano lid much as in the final work. It is singled out with an arrow and the notation "use". At this point, a second figure stands in the back middle ground, arms upraised. On the 22nd and 23rd, in drawings annotated with measurements and words including "reflections in window" and "reflections", the second figure becomes the mirrored image of the *Singer*.

One of the primary functions of format in Colville's work is to objectify and fix the limits of a scene. When we represent things in the interior forum of the imagination, it is our experience of these things, what we know and feel about them, how we have judged their connectedness to us, that conditions how they appear as images and how they associate with other things. Mental images are therefore not so much shapes to which we subsequently attach meaning and value as they are embodiments of our sentiments and knowledge of their worth. As our attention focusses on certain aspects of the mental picture, they become relatively clear and delineated, but the rest is relegated for the moment to a hazy background, an indeterminate depth from which more visual information can be summoned by our need or desire. We can linger for some time with an inescapable image, the face of a lover, perhaps, or an object of fear, but when our attention moves about from one feature of a mental representation to another, each of these features comes into focus, holds its position for a moment, and drops once again into that invisible reservoir of potential imagery which is our memory. More constellations of visual characteristics than stable, determined scenes, images projected in the imagination appear within indefinite, changeable limits. When Colville experiments with the format of a picture in his drawings, it is as if he were using a rational tool external to the mental representation to stabilize its limits and to establish an efficacious, objective frame of reference in which the imagination can continue its work. The format he finally chooses is, then, while appropriate, neither a simple given nor a necessary condition of the originating mental image; it is a tool deliberately fashioned to work out the implications of the image during the subsequent construction of the picture.

A drawing Colville made of *Couple on Bridge* specifically for inclusion in a textbook illustrates his use of format and surface division. Drawn on 18 January 1993, that is, after the process of image construction was completed, it presents a stable view of the final arrangement. There are two images on the page: the one above, a scale drawing of the painting; the one below, an example of Le Corbusier's Modulor with notations of the measurements in the painting. The painting is square and the Modulor is a horizontal rectangle; examining this discrepancy, what becomes clear is that Colville has used the Modulor directly for only the upper part of the bridge from the road top to where the girders are cut off by the upper framing edge and has truncated the right-hand side of the Modulor with the right framing edge. But nothing in this application is haphazard. The 50-degree angle of the girder rising from the roadbed at the left corresponds to the angle which bisects the lower left corner of the Modulor construction. The divisions of the Modulor determine the placement of the main figures, which are separated by the narrow segment to the right of the place of the right angle. The proportions set up by the main divisions are those of the Fibonacci series (3, 5, 8, 13, 21 and 34), and justify both the truncation of the Modulor to the right – the distance from the upright beam to the picture's edge is an 8 in the series – and the proportions of the rectangle formed between the roadbed and the bottom of the picture. The centre of this lower rectangle is the vanishing point, tying the depth structure of the pictorial space to the picture's surface pattern.

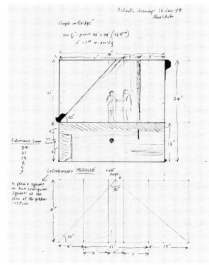

9.12

When examining a finished work, it could appear that the geometric interpretation has been imposed upon the image from outside to create a system of formal relationships. Sometimes, this seems all the more true in that it is possible to find more than one geometric model to fit the spacing of the image, and none of these is necessarily the one used by the artist. But this approach misses the point. Colville uses geometry to discover and display *expressive* relationships between the various visual elements that make up the image: the exact positioning of parts, the amount of surface area they occupy, the intervals between them, their role in the rhythmic flow of the totality. From this geometrically ponderated positioning comes the pervasive sense of necessity characteristic of Colville's work. It is true that, after the fact, alternative patterns can be found. This is because the figures of plane geometry belong to the same family of forms and, being closely related, are subject to cognate rules of shape, production, inscription and segmentation. What is important here is how the geometry works in regard to Colville's originating idea-image. At a certain moment in the drawing process, he casts a possible geometric form like a net over the image, trying to capture the shapes, at least tentatively, in a pattern of intervals. Sometimes this gives results early, as if he had already intuited the adequation of the geometric forms to the subject matter; in other cases, alternatives are attempted until the proper coincidence of geometry and subject occurs. Once the general pattern is established, subsequent adjustments are made until final working drawings fix the details. Few, if any, changes are made to the geometric plan during the process of painting the image.

A good illustration of Colville's approach to geometry is found in the sequence of drawings for *Chaplain.* Two rough sketches on one small sheet of heavy white paper dated 25 April 1991 show views of the pulpit in almost square formats; the pulpit occupies most of the space, and the Chaplain's head is behind and below the horizontal railing of the platform. One is annotated with "lower eye level", the other with "standing eye level". On 8 and 9 May, Colville made several life drawings. Of those devoted to the pulpit and the corner of the church, one is diagrammatic, giving details on the height of eye level, the distance to the nearest corner, the level of the stone floor and a notation concerning a position "10 cm., o.c." There are also drawings of the Chaplain seated – one in full view, another behind a spindleless version of the pulpit – and a closer image of his head and shoulders. For these, Colville's chaplain friend from Acadia University served as the model. Between 10 and 16 May, geometric studies were overlaid in different colours of ink on one of the seated *Chaplain* drawings of the 9th. At this point extensions of the original square sketched format take place – a narrow vertical band to the right and a rectangle to the left. The geometric work centres on the original square and produces the new format and distribution of parts by progressive inscriptions of related circles, squares, diamonds and an octagon. This "architecture" of the pictorial space appears, without the Chaplain, on a drawing worked and reworked on 22 and 31 May and 3, 4 and 13 June. On 3 and 4 June, a scale drawing without subject matter shows the integration of the perspective system with the geometric pattern. During and following the period of geometric elaboration, life drawings were made detailing, for example, the Chaplain's hands and shoes and architectural features of the church.

Photocopies were used to work out *Western Star.* There are, as mentioned above, the early appearances of the tourist with a camera associated with studies for *Taxi* and *Köln Express.* One of these, dated 27 February 1985, shows two figures, unframed, at the lower right-hand corner of the page, the person with the camera facing frontward, angled to the left, taking a picture of the other, seen in a sketchy side view. On the 28th, a page of drawings was executed showing trucks in relatively large scale at oblique angles to the picture plane. The man with the camera appears twice inside the framed truck images and once, in side view and slightly bent at the hips, outside the frames. By 6 July, the image had firmed up to some degree and is associated with a geometric drawing, including measurements, of a circle inscribed within a square, a diamond within the circle, and the upper half of the square subdivided into a long band and two vertical rectangles at either side of a centrally located square. The left-hand vertical rectangle is subdivided into a square and a rectangle, which itself is subdivided in a process of embedding. The two sketches on the page show the same two personages: the one with the camera, in side view, is bending slightly at the hips; the other, being photographed, is positioned back to

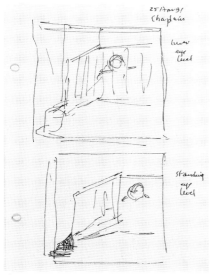

18.01

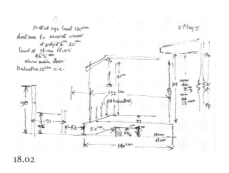

18.02

18.11

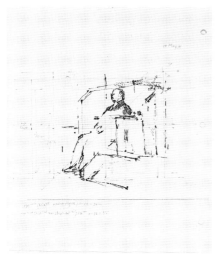

18.09

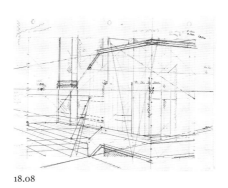

18.08

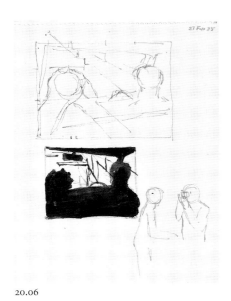

20.06

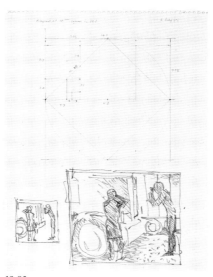

19.02

the viewer, angled towards the right. But in one sketch the right arm is lifted to the head, in the other, the left. On 10 and 11 July, a sketch and the geometric construction are shown combined as if in overlay. The man takes his position in the far right quarter, and the other figure, left arm lifted, in the second quarter to the right of the left edge. Eye level is noted, and the difference in height between a Mack and a Ford truck is indicated. On the 24th and 27th, though the same overall pattern is used, the man's height has been modified, and it becomes clear that the narrow band at the top has been extended around the whole picture, creating a border framing a central square. A woman stands on the border, and it separates the man from the right framing edge. From this point on, photocopies are put to work. A drawing, apparently from 29 July, in which the figures of the man and woman are embodied with some detail, was photocopied for work on 9 August. Another copy of the same image, dated the 12th, appears with different modifications. Additional detailed studies of the figures were made subsequent to these determinations, for example, the work done on 18 September which shows the man's figure in relationship to the picture's grid structure at half actual size.

Although for the most part the development of a geometric pattern proceeds by intensification and adjustment, with *Traveller* there was a false start. Through mid-February 1992, Colville attempted to organize the horizontal rectangle of the picture by developing a pattern of circles and semicircles based on the steering wheel and perhaps the dials of the dashboard. From 6 to 24 February, sketches show his efforts to place significant parts of the image – the traveller, the rearview mirror, the steering wheel, eye level – in various arrangements of abutting or slightly overlapping circles, some extending downward outside the picture's edge. On the 24th and 25th, a new approach introduces the large concentric semicircles that, in the drawings of 26, 27 and 28 February, bring the bridge, traveller and rearview mirror together, with the steering wheel as a centre. With adjustments still to be made – the rearview mirror is too large and too far to the right, the traveller is too bulky, and the outline of the hill in the background is still somewhat undetermined – the acrylic drawing of 2 March embodies this new approach to the image.

The system of perspective adopted for each picture seems to be keyed primarily to the general disposition of the originating idea-image and subsequently organized and correlated with the surface pattern. In those instances in which a seascape appears early in the development, the pictured horizon line acts as eye level, one of the critical elements in the construction of pictorial depth. When the position of the horizon is less evident, eye level is frequently indicated as soon as the image starts to take shape, though it is still subject to variation in conjunction with other changes. In the case of *Couple on Bridge,* the sequence done on 7 June 1992, only five days after the rough sketches of the 1st and 2nd, shows both the eye level under the

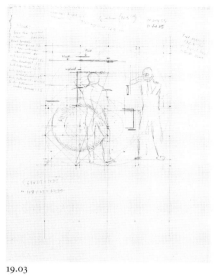

19.03

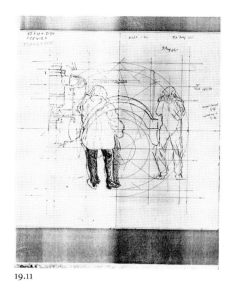

19.11

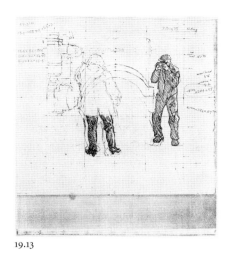

19.13

19.14

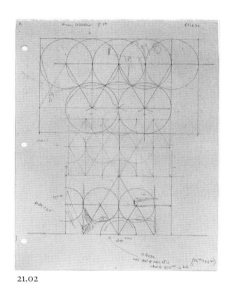

21.02

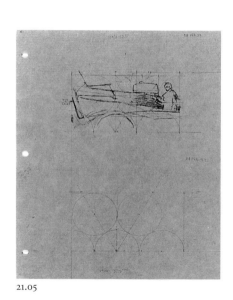

21.05

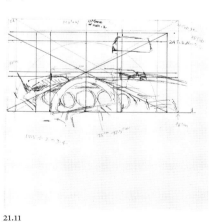

21.11

21.15

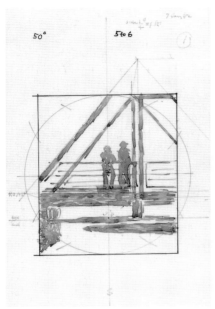

9.04

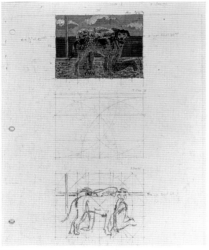

13.09

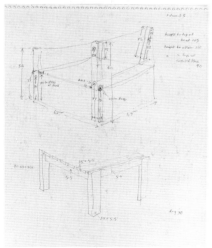

8.02

bridge and the position of the vanishing point. These remain stable in the subsequent elaboration of the image. In another sequence, the drawings for *Dog and Groom* dated 30 September 1990 show the horizon in line with the dog's eyes; on 2 October, this line is used to set up measuring points (marked "M1" and "M2"), and on 3 and 4 January 1991, it is explicitly labelled as eye level. However, by 14 February, following the shift of the scene indoors, the level is raised so that it corresponds with the groom's eyes. The drawings for *Verandah* dated from 1 to 15 June 1983 show how the detailed diagrammatic drawings of the chairs are integrated into the double perspective system used to construct the final image. In a similar manner, a faxed drawing dated 24 April 1989 indicates some of the details in the artist's development of the perspective for *Woman on Diving Board.*

Although the purpose of authentication is to confirm the likelihood of a picture in regard to the everyday world, the information required can be introduced at various points during the process of image development, even, as with the diagrammatic drawing for *French Cross,* several years before the image-idea takes final shape. The measurements given on the diagrammatic sketches – for example details of the church corner and pulpit for *Chaplain* – serve in the calculation of relative distances and sizes of things in conjunction with the system of perspective being used. For *Boat and Bather,* the same type of information is noted on a photocopy of a publication presenting the features of the Drascombe Scaffie. When working on *Couple on Bridge,* Colville measured the actual bridge and discovered that the sloping girder rose at an angle of 50 degrees, exactly that required for the lower corner of the Modulor construction. A happy coincidence.

Photography plays an important role in the process of authentication, both to verify the general disposition of the figurative elements and to focus on appropriate detail. The photocopy of photographs for *Taxi* dated 21 and 28 March 1985 is concerned with what is seen from the back seat of a car with the driver on the right. The photographs for *Singer* focus on the tilt of the various models' heads and in some cases, the shape of their mouths. The Polaroid photo taken for *French Cross* on 27 July 1988 shows the twist of the rider's body at the waist and the turn of her head with the notation "head turned more". Perhaps the most interesting example in this vein is the photocollage of the view from the driver's seat for *Traveller.* The view is so wide that no standard camera could take it in with a single image, nor could a driver's eyes focus on much of it all at once. The information had to be recorded in several photographs, which were pieced together as one view – an impossible view. Paradoxically, in confirming the visual consistency of the image, the process of authentication moves the picture away from perceptual verisimilitude by placing the viewer-as-driver in the peculiar situation of focussing on a vanishing point in the presence of clear visual information that should be blurry.

Sometime during the development of an image-idea, Colville makes a decision about whether the picture will be a painting or a serigraph. Producing an average of three finished works a year, one factor in his decision is external to the image: he likes to change from one medium to the other, so if he has just done two paintings, it is likely that he will choose to do a print. There are, no doubt, internal factors that come into play as well. Prints require a mechanical overlay of colours that is not conducive to certain effects that can be obtained with the paintbrush – the luminescent sky of *Couple on Bridge,* for example, or the glow of the car's lights in *Kiss with Honda.* Until the decision about medium is made, however, the process of image development is the same for the paintings and the serigraphs.

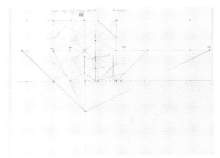

8.04

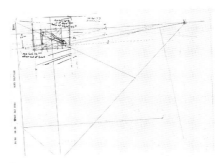

6.04

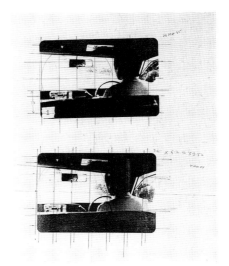

20.11

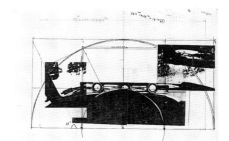

21.08

B. CHURCH AND HORSE

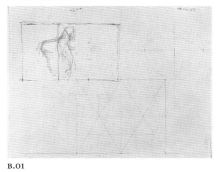

B.01

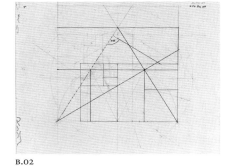

B.02

B.04

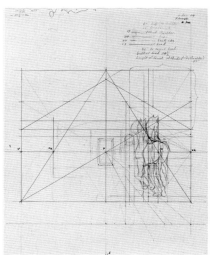

B.05

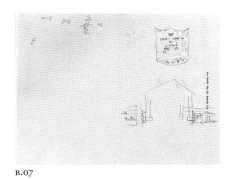

B.07

1. ARRIVAL

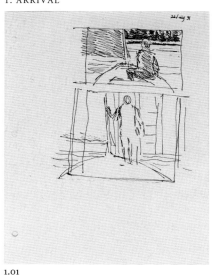

1.01

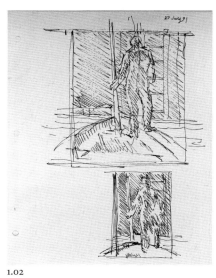

1.02

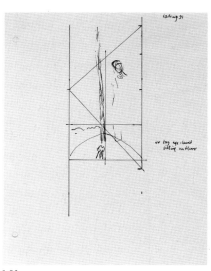

1.03

118

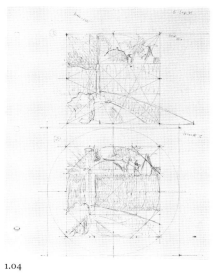

1.04

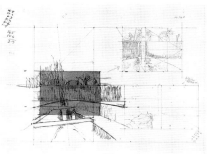

1.05

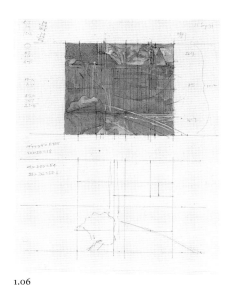

1.06

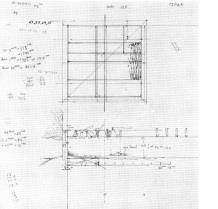

1.07

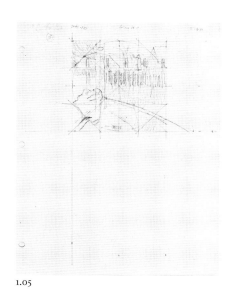

1.08

2. LOOKING DOWN

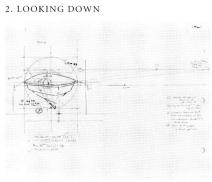

2.04

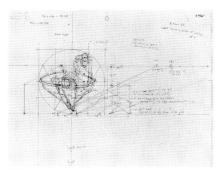

2.05

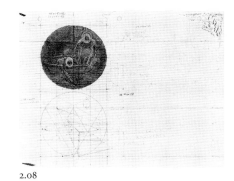

2.08

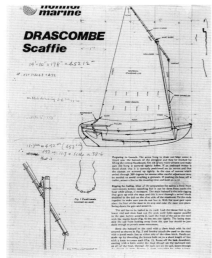

3.01

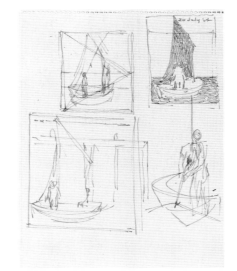

3.03

3.04

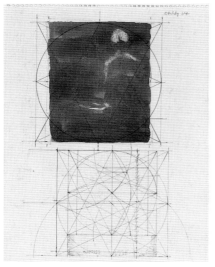

3.05

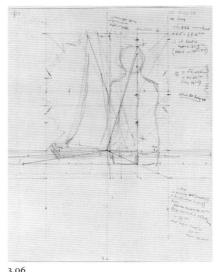

3.06

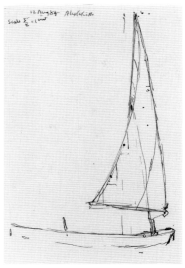

3.07

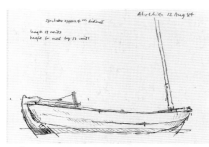

3.08

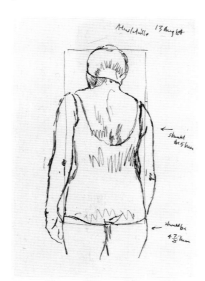

3.09

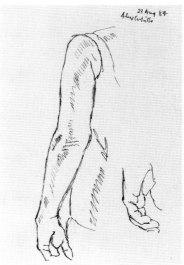

3.11

4. LOW TIDE

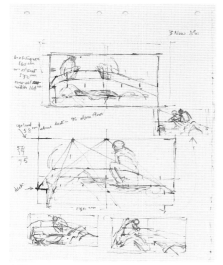

4.02

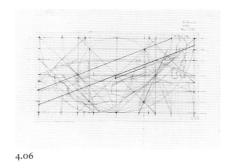

4.06

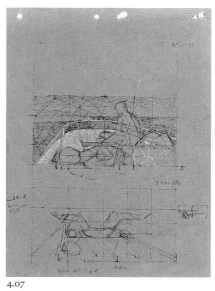

4.07

5. FLOATING WOMAN

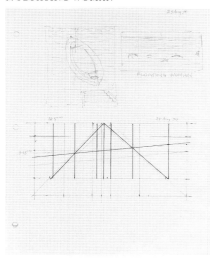

5.01

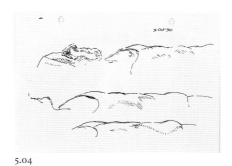

5.04

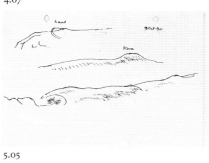

5.05

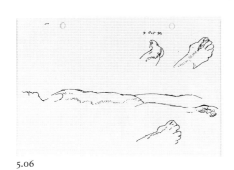

5.06

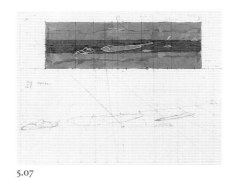

5.07

6. WOMAN ON DIVING BOARD

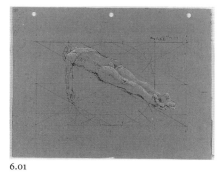

6.01

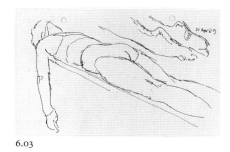

6.03

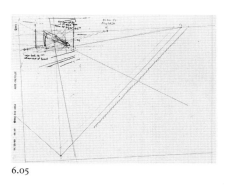

6.05

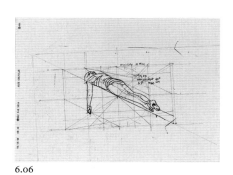

6.06

7. WHITE CANOE

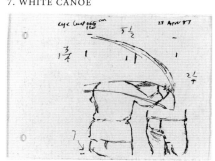

7.01

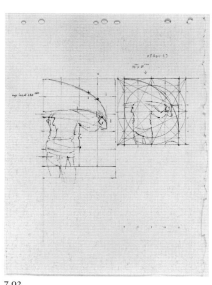

7.02

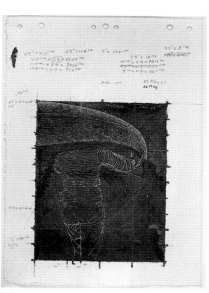

7.05

8. VERANDAH

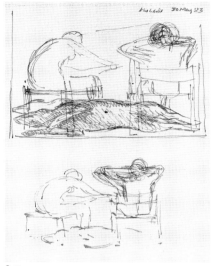

8.01

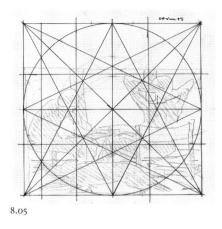

8.05

8.07

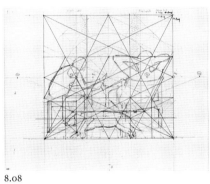

8.08

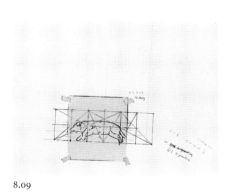

8.09

9. COUPLE ON BRIDGE

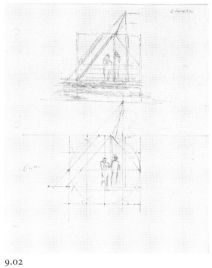

9.02

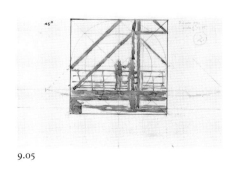

9.05

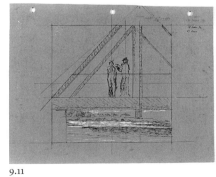

9.11

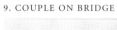

9.08

10. TARGET SHOOTING

10.01

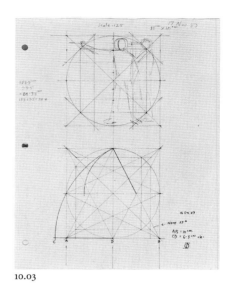

10.02

10.03

10.04

10.06

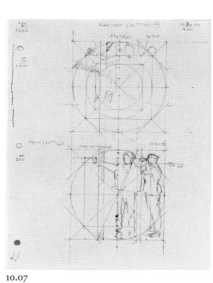

10.07

11. WOMAN WITH REVOLVER

11.01

11.02

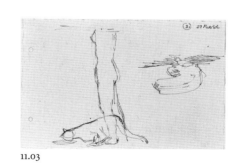

11.03

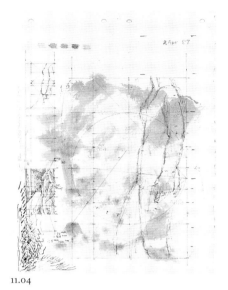

11.04

11.05

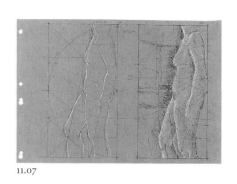

11.07

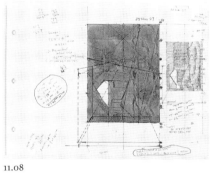

11.08

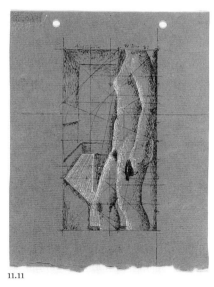

11.11

12. CAT AND DOG

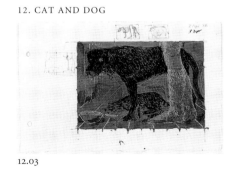

12.03

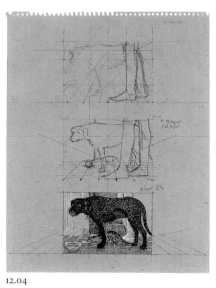

12.04

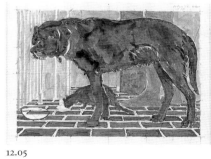

12.05

13. DOG AND GROOM

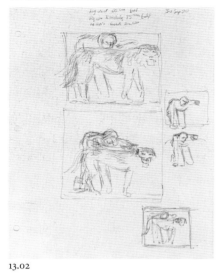

13.02

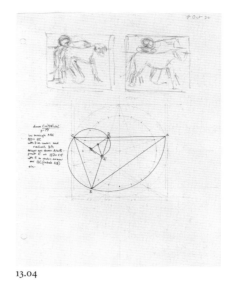

13.04

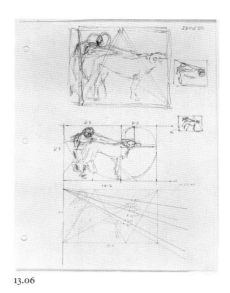

13.06

13.07

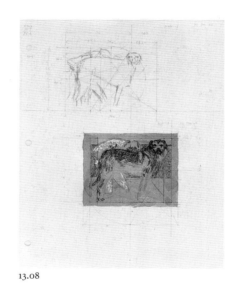

13.08

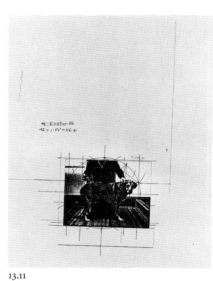

13.11

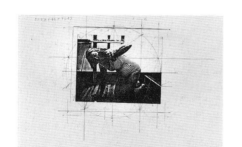

13.12

14. BAT

14.01

14.05

15.06

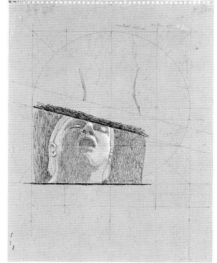

15.08

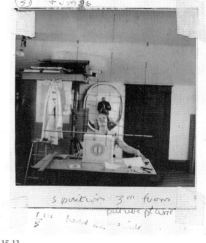

15.09

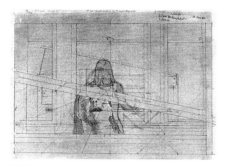

15.10

15.11

15.13

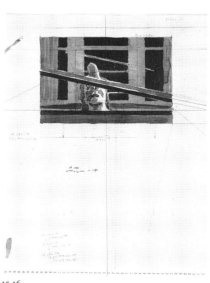

15.14

15.15

15.16

15.17

15.18

15.19

16. HORSE AND GIRL

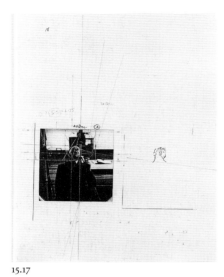

16.03

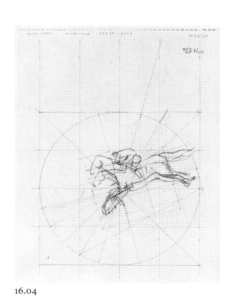

16.04

16.05

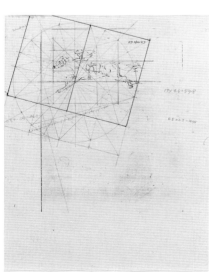

16.07

17.02

17.03

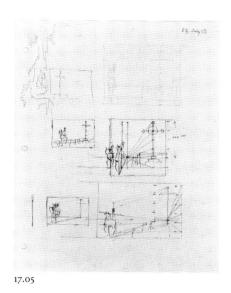

17.05

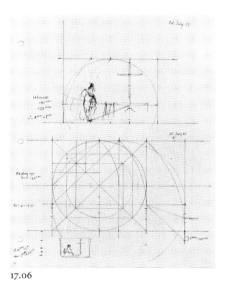

17.06

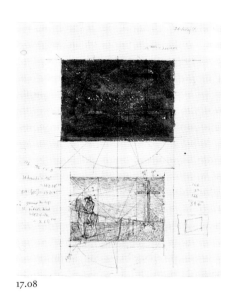

17.08

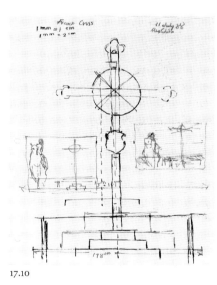

17.10

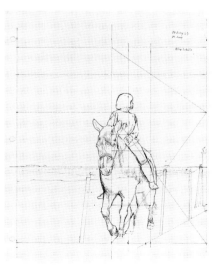

17.11

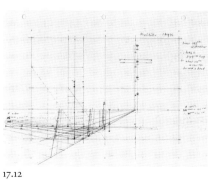

17.12

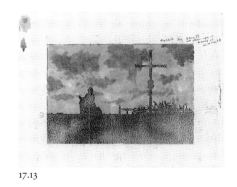

17.13

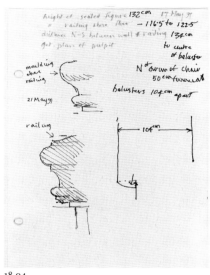

18.04

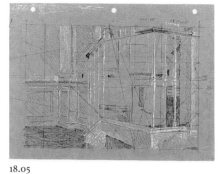

18.05

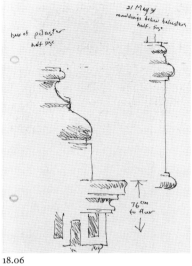

18.06

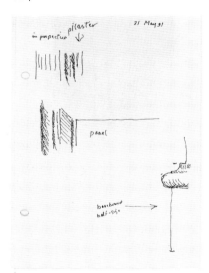

18.07

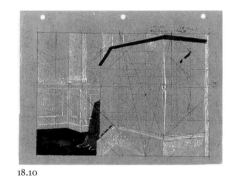

18.10

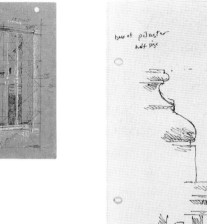

18.12

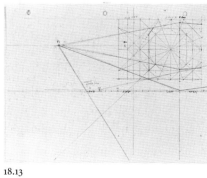

18.13

19. WESTERN STAR

19.05

19.08

19.09

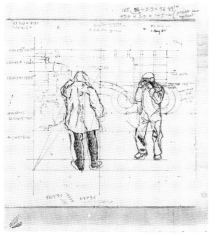

19.10

19.12

20. TAXI

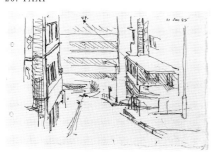

20.04

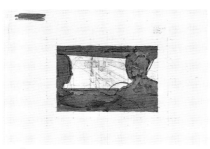

20.08

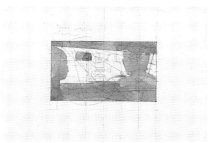

20.10

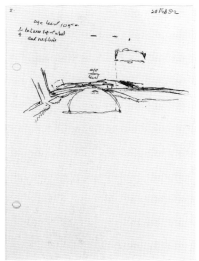

21.01

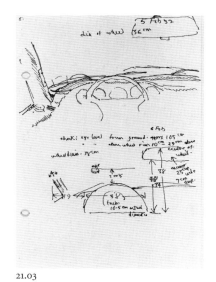

21.03

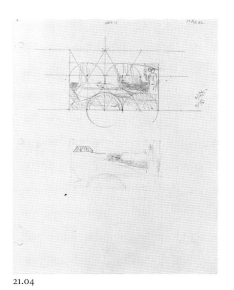

21.04

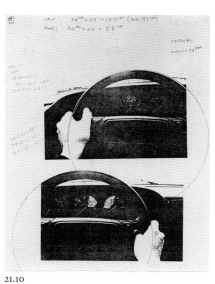

21.06

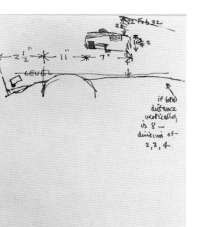

21.07

21.09

21.10

21.14

21.16

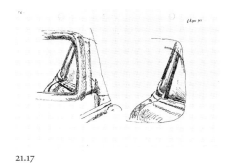

21.17

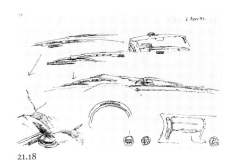

21.18

0. KISS WITH HONDA

0.01

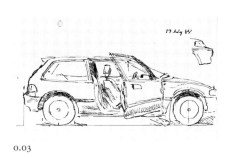

0.03

0.04

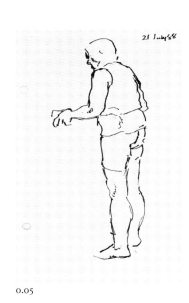

0.05

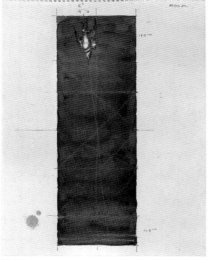

23.04

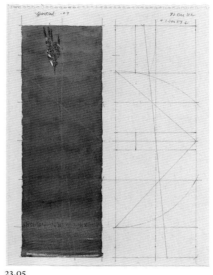

23.05

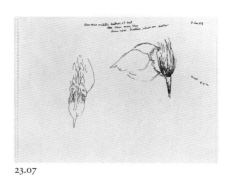

23.07

23.08

23.09

24. RAT

24.02

24.04

24.05

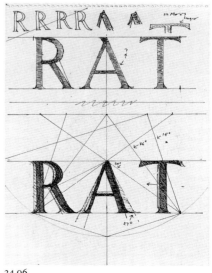

24.06

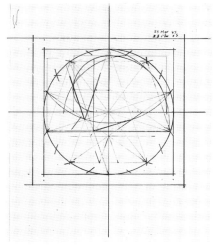

24.07

24.08

24.09

24.10

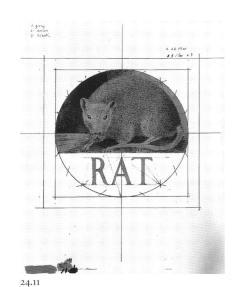

24.11

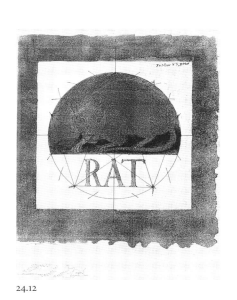

24.12

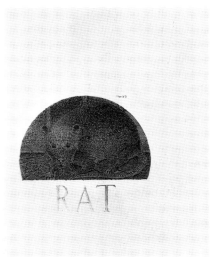

24.13

24.14

24.15

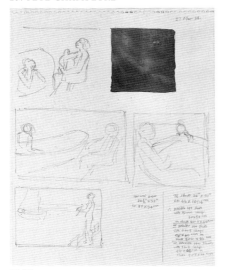

25.02

25.03

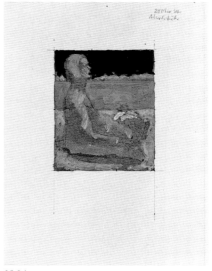

25.04

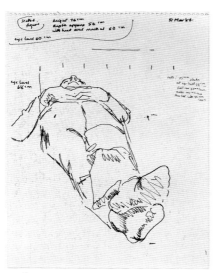

25.06

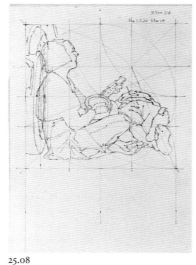

25.08

25.10

26. BELL BUOY AND CORMORANT

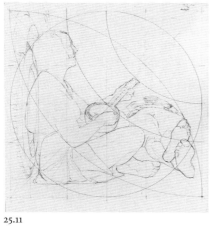

25.11

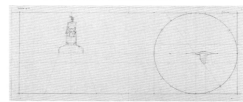

26.04

27.04

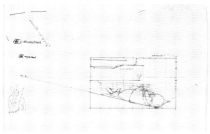

27.07

27.08

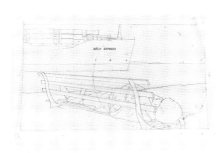

27.09

27.10

27.11

27.12

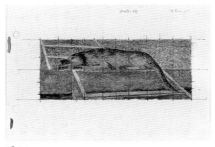

28.04

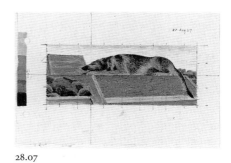

28.06

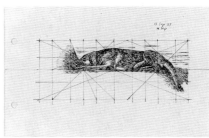

28.07

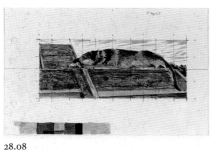

28.08

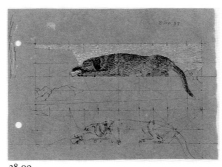

28.09

28.10

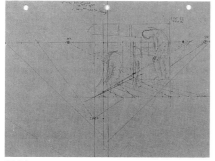

29.04

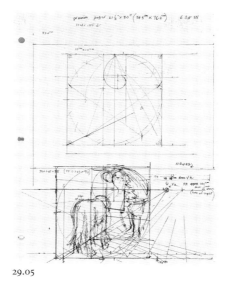

29.05

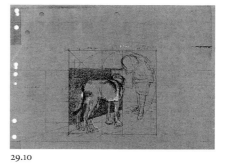

29.06

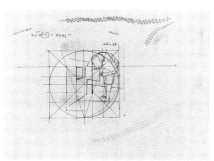

29.08

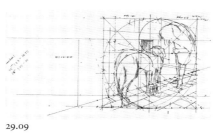

29.09

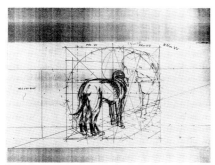

29.10

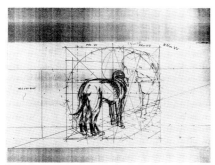

29.11

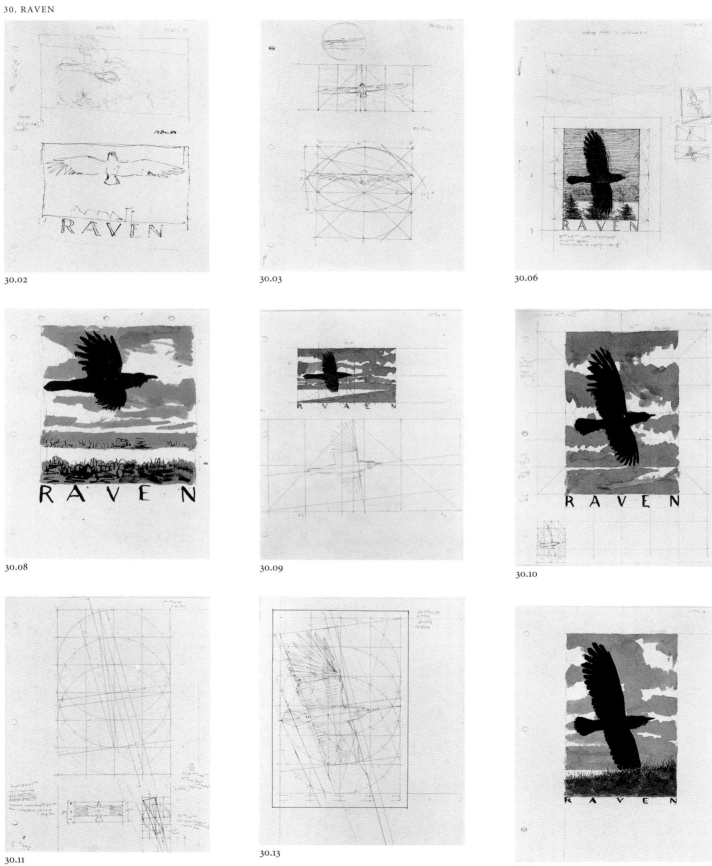

30.02

30.03

30.06

30.08

30.09

30.10

30.11

30.13

30.14

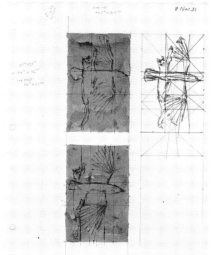

32.03

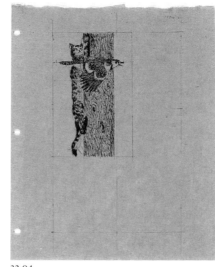

32.04

32.05

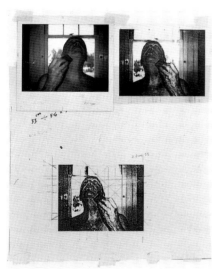

32.09

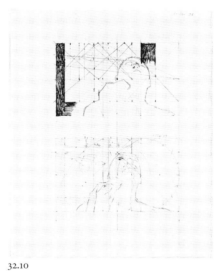

32.10

32.11

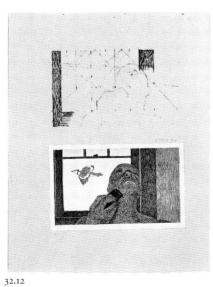

32.12

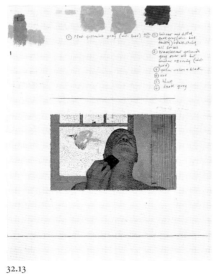

32.13

32.14

32.15

32.16

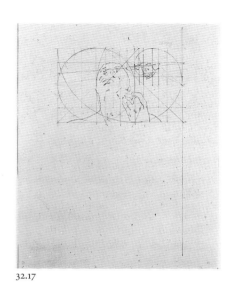

32.17

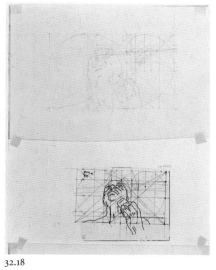

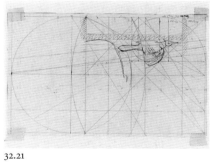

32.18

32.19

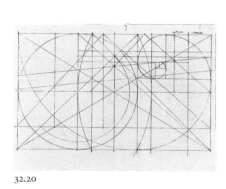

32.20

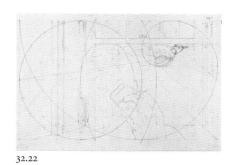

32.21

32.22

32.23

32.24

32.25

32.26

32.27

The Prints

There are ten silk-screen prints, also called serigraphs, in the exhibition. They hang in the gallery to the right of the paintings and are displayed in conjunction with a selection of relevant drawings and, in one case, examples of various stages in the preparation of the print image. The purpose of this arrangement, unlike that, primarily contemplative, used for the paintings, is to allow the viewer to enter into the process of the print's production as well as to interact with the final work. It is hoped that this approach will also have a didactic value, especially for those who wish to work on their own sense of image construction.

Serigraphy is a development of the stencil process through which images are formed by layering individual colour patterns one upon another in a predetermined sequence until the total image is built up. What distinguishes serigraphy from simple cutout stencils is the use of a silk screen stretched over a frame to hold the image pattern as an arrangement of nonporous (or negative) areas, which resist the passage of ink, and porous (or positive) areas, through which the ink passes to be distributed onto the paper's surface. With this process, the various layers of the image can be drawn directly onto the screen, produced with stencil cutouts, or reproduced from previously prepared drawings of each layer of the image-pattern through a photomechanical system.

The photomechanical system is the one used by Alex Colville. Once he has decided that an image will be a print rather than a painting, he works it out to its final compositional state and analyzes it into appropriate colour layers, each of which calls for its own drawing set out to exact scale. Using a vacuum table, these drawings are then printed on a light-sensitive film. When this film is washed, it becomes a stencil which is applied to a screen and registered with guide marks to ensure that it falls exactly in place during printing. Colville, who does even the more mechanical aspects of the printing himself, produces a group of artist's proofs and a run of seventy numbered prints of each image.

Diving from the upper edge of the image, a kingfisher plummets vertiginously down the surface of a vertical root-9 rectangle, half-folded wings set back rigidly for its swift trajectory through space, speed-swept crest held close against its head in the streaming air, pointed beak pointing at its prey far below. Set close to the picture plane, the bird's plunging shape and the patterned flow of the white bands in its blue-grey, black and orange-beige plumage, project it in sharp relief against the languid horizontal drifts of warmer and softer tones which compose the cloud-strewn sky, the sea and a narrow peninsula. From a source below the lower edge of the image, parallel waves lap into the picture, suggesting the location of the bird's target. In the most minute and critical ways – calculation of distance, adjustment of body and feathers, control of angle of descent and speed, estimation of impact time – the bird has accorded itself to its prey. Its flight pattern has been set and the action has begun. The bird is committed to its pursuit. And now, only time, those very moments which are absent from the picture, can determine the outcome.

This picture, though literal in its representation of the bird, can be understood metaphorically, much like the painting *Target Shooting*, as an image of carefully assumed purposefulness. The format of the work, the angle at which the kingfisher plunges, and the shape and scale of the bird in contrast to the generalized segment of landscape have all been worked out to emphasize the adequation of the seeker to its goal: aiming, trying to attain an objective, involves measuring oneself against the target, sorting out and assimilating information, making adjustments, learning to identify with what first appeared to be an independent external object. In the quest, subject and object, knower and known, become one.

The upper images on a page of drawings dated 5 November 1982 show the kingfisher in side view, rocketing in an almost perfect diagonal from the top left-hand corner towards the bottom right-hand corner of a vertical rectangle; to the left of these images is written the sign for root-3, indicating the format under consideration. The angle is dynamic and maximizes the distance between the bird and its objective, but apparently not enough for the artist. There are three more sketches on the page, two showing the kingfisher at the moment it interrupts its horizontal flight and begins to fold into the dive, the other showing the back and both wings of the plunging bird; the bird has moved towards the upper centre of the image and is now out of line with the top left-hand corner. At least in one case, the height of the format has increased and its proportional width narrowed, providing more distance for the bird's descent. The next day, three sketches deal explicitly with questions of angle, position and proportion. The image at the top left shows a vertical rectangle in which have been inscribed Le Corbusier's Modulor and a semicircle (its centre point on the right edge directly opposite the place of the right angle). Based on two

In 1971 my wife and I were walking our dog Shasta on a beach on the Atlantic coast of Denmark. We saw a jet fighter (long pointed nose, swept-back wings) diving toward the sea, practising combat. My "Kingfisher" was done twelve years later. Nature imitates art, as Oscar Wilde said, and in this case art in the image of a bird, imitates a machine.

Alex Colville, "Remarks", November 1993

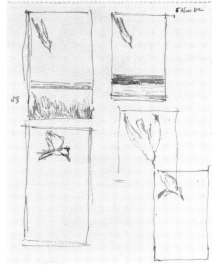

23.01

145

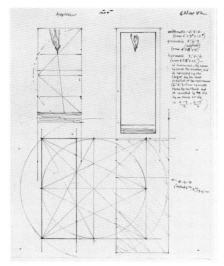

23.02

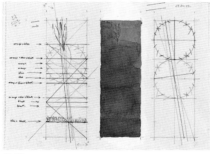

23.03

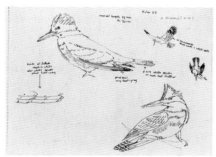

23.06

vertically contiguous squares, this construction provides increased diving space and, using the points at which the inscribed right angle cuts the edges of the Modulor's "located" third square, a geometrically derived angle of descent. The drawing to the top right increases the height of the format by using three full squares to form a vertical root-9 rectangle. The width of the format has narrowed proportionally and the scale of the bird is relatively smaller, but the angle of descent seems to remain constant. To the right of this image there is a note dealing with arithmetic, geometric and harmonic proportions, suggesting that the artist is considering how to determine the divisions and sizes involved in the picture's composition. The lower drawing is a geometric exercise employing the sequence 4–6–9, from which the 12-by-4-cm rectangle announced at the top of the page can be derived.

The drawings dated from 29 December 1982 through 18 January 1983 show the artist working on adjustments of various features within what has become a stable root-9 format. The first page of this group of studies shows, at the left, proportional divisions of the rectangle based on a triple Modulor construction to set squares at the places of the right angle within the three contiguous squares constituting the format. The divisions are indicated with colour notations. The angle of the bird's dive, also derived from the Modulor, is noted as 9 degrees, and the lowest division at the bottom suggests land or a horizon dividing sky from sea. Subsequently, there are studies varying or elaborating upon the basic geometric structure, and these are accompanied by sketches in coloured washes. On 9 January, for example, the bird's angle of descent is noted as 6 degrees, indicating that even this highly important feature is still being explored. In the midst of these geometric considerations, on 3 January 1983, the artist prepared diagrammatic sketches of the kingfisher, both perched and in flight, that include details about its feathers and colour pattern. The processes of embodiment and authentication were already under way.

The fish, the object of this quest for an exact adequation of form, does not have to be depicted: it is present in the bird's position and attitude.

23. KINGFISHER, 1983

Serigraph, XI/XLII
96.6 x 33 cm
Numbered, signed, dated
David & Marilyn Burnett collection, Toronto

I was once on the breakwater of our cottage when a rat emerged from the rocks and stood, looking at me. He, or she, was very impressive: bright clear eyes, fine healthy coat, quick, decisive actions.

Alex Colville, "Remarks", November 1993

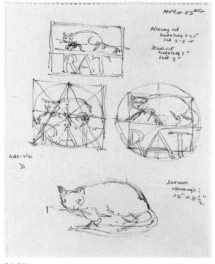

24.01

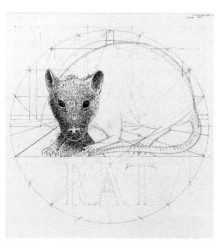

24.03

Pausing an instant as it notices that we are here, the rat stiffens its muscles imperceptibly, turns its head slightly, juts its muzzle a bit forward and, focussing its attention on our eyes, wreaks the havoc of blind midnight in our hearts. Crouched in the truncated circle which is its pictorial habitat, its arched brown back spiralling gently away from the curved edge of its niche, its tail brought around close to the body, its claws tingling with deft intelligence, the rat is alert, aware and in harmony with its surroundings. It is contained and self-contained, in control, invulnerable. See the knowledge staring out from those black depths? See the ruthless calculation, the determination, the wisdom of the survivor? As we choke on our garbage, the rat eats it. Do we not respond with disgust and loathing? Do we not need to escape this presence, to distance it, to reify it with a label? It is there, the name of what we see, placed with simple elegance under the animal. And though it is redundant, redundant and reverberating like a scream of awareness, we utter it with our lips, we spell it out: R-A-T. The word censures animal. We growl the "r", we spit the "t". Its pronunciation somehow satisfies us – RAT, rat, r-a-t – and pushes the beast away from the place where the panic rises in our bellies. But now, think. Is our fear really about the animal, or does it concern what terrifies us in ourselves?

The preparatory sketches for *Rat* drawn on 14 March 1983 show Colville's consideration of possible formats as well as his interest in the circle, the triangle and the star. The circle, at this point, could be inscribed in a square or become the format itself. By 16 and 17 March, the letters "RAT" were lettered roughly on the base line of various geometric figures inscribed within the circle. Subsequent work around the 20th led to the preparation of an undated Mylar overlay of the rat and the linear structure of its surroundings, and another overlay, dated March 23, in which the final geometric structure was set down. Meanwhile, on the 21st, studies detailing especially the head and mouth of the Norway rat were made from a scientific book, and on the 22nd, the graphic characteristics for the lettering of the word "RAT" and its exact placement in the circle came under consideration. From 23 March to about 4 April, an extensive series of photocopies of the Mylar overlays was prepared and used for colour studies leading up to colour selection for the print.

The recession of the floorboards draws our eyes to the vanishing point behind the rat's snout, just below its pitch-black stare. We are held in this uncanny mutual gaze, uncomfortable, our blood refrigerated by a premonition of what is to come.

RAT

Alex Colville 1983 45/70

24. RAT, 1983

Serigraph, 45/70
32.9 x 33 cm
Numbered, signed, dated
Courtesy of the Drabinsky Gallery, Toronto

*There is a great painting of this title which
I always thought was a Giorgione, but I
recently discovered is a Titian. I use the
title as homage to the painting.
The woman is giving forth; the man
is recumbent, taking it in.*

Alex Colville, "Remarks", November 1993

This is an intimate festival, the delight of a quiet woodland clearing, still, full of gentle song and repose. Separating a relaxed couple from dense green forest beyond, pale grey-blue waters fold upon themselves in slender, tenuous waves, barely murmuring their secret meditations. The wheel and fender of a truck angle into the scene from the left like a wall, closing the space on that side and framing, with the waters and trees behind, the space of the couple's peaceful celebration. She sits cross-legged, her draped earthen-coloured skirts revealing her knees and bare foot; her upright back is turned to the wheel but, as if in a self-assured gesture of independence, does not lean on it. She strums the banjo she holds diagonally, pointing its neck across the clearing. Chin lifted slightly, face and legs suffused with glowing light, she sings some soft song to the sun. He lies on his back, the soles of his bare feet facing the viewer, his body angled towards the centre of the picture. His hands are clasped on his stomach; his head is not visible from our vantage point. Enveloped in the sunlight, he listens in tranquil rapture to her song or perhaps has already slipped away to that serene, resonant place where music and the flow of the waters are one.

Intense work on the drawings for *Fête champêtre* took place at the end of March and the beginning of April 1984. On a page dated 27 March, a sketch shows the woman very close to the picture plane, her body cropped at the hips by the lower framing edge, her back apparently leaning against a large lumpy object while the man, it would seem, lies stretched out horizontally in the middle ground, in the place finally occupied by the water. On the same page, however, there is another drawing on a brown wash showing the man lying at the approximate angle found in the finished work. These two drawings are formatted in vertical rectangles. A third drawing on the page is a geometric study dividing the format into various angles, curves and segments; though the given format is a square, one of the divisions forms a vertical rectangle of proportions which correspond to measurements inscribed above the diagram. By 30 March the square format and the scale of the image are set. In the drawings from that day, it is clear how the angles at which the man lies and the banjo is held have been determined geometrically, but subsequently the plan for the banjo will change. There is also some question about the eye level to be used to construct the work's perspective. In the drawing dated 3, 4 and 5 April, the banjo is aligned on the square's diagonal, and eye level is set at the height of the woman's chin. The man's face, though it appears on the study of 31 March, is no longer visible. There also seems to have been some doubt about the use of the truck's wheel to frame the left side of the image, an important decision, because the way the wheel encloses the space has much to do with the work's feeling of intimacy. On 28 March the wheel is absent, but by the 30th it is a major element of the construction. On 9, 10 and 11 April, Colville drew the image to the actual size of the print.

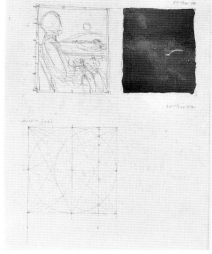

25.01

25. FÊTE CHAMPÊTRE, 1984

Serigraph, 44/70
54 x 50.7 cm
Numbered, signed, dated
Mary Pratt collection, Terre-Neuve

Complemented by the angles of the truck tire and the recumbent man which open the scene towards the front, the picture's vanishing point invites us to share this couple's company. They know us so well, these two, that they will continue their reverie undisturbed. And we, very still now, can almost hear the hushed harmonics of peace in this gentle festival. A perfectly silent music happens then in our hearts.

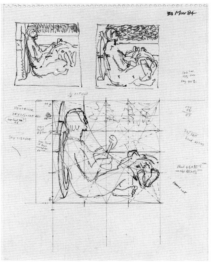

25.05

25.07

25.09

Profiled in stark relief against a sullen, cloud-banked sky and the wide expanse of a grey-green sea, two solitary figures, each isolated, each independent, each self-contained, pursue their respective purposes. From the right, on the horizontal median of the image, a cormorant flies parallel to the picture plane, neck extended full length, hooked beak pointing straight ahead. The horizon line is about the same distance above the bird's tail as the tips of its flight feathers are below. The stream-lined black bird seems determined to follow its course through the mid-foreground of the picture; unless it should choose to alter its direction, it will fly on without encountering the other object in the scene. The bell buoy, emerging from the sea on the horizontal median of the picture, floats to the left, noticeably farther away from its side of the image than the bird is from the right edge. Rising above the curved surfaces of the floating tank from just below the horizon, a scaffold serves as the housing for a bell and the support for a lamp. The bell buoy, farther back in the scene than the cormorant, marks a location and suggests relative distances, especially the gap between it and the cormorant. Defined by their isolated shapes, by their figurative closure, the bell buoy and the cormorant will never meet, never close the inexorable gap between them.

The sense of independence and isolation evoked by this print has much to do with the exact relative placement of the figures according to geometric and mathematical divisions discernible in some of the preparatory drawings. An early sketch in ink and acrylic washes dated 23 July 1984 gives a rough version of the format – a rectangle overlaid with a half-circle and tentatively subdivided into three sections – and the general layout of the picture. This is given a much more precise rendition on 30 November, when the rectangle is divided into a square at the right from which the geometric sequence of root-2 to root-7 rectangles is produced. The framing edge at the left falls just inside the place where the root-6 arc cuts the bottom edge, making the format slightly less than a perfect root-6 rectangle. The cormorant's neck intersects the vertical median of the original square, its body centred on the horizontal median of the picture. The bell buoy's position corresponds to the root-4 division of the surface and floats on the horizontal median, lining up its level of emergence from the water with the bird's beak. There are other divisions of the surface which appear motivated by proportional or mathematical concerns and which provide a reason for the slight truncation of the format at the left: between the root-2 and root-3 arcs, a vertical line and the left, top and bottom framing edges form a square equal to the originating square to the right, and this same vertical line, when paired with the line dropping past the point of the bird's beak, forms, again with the top and bottom of the picture, another square of the same size. A sequence of numbers written at the top of the drawing dated 2 December – a proportional progres-

Cormorants fly close to the water, thus gaining aerodynamic efficiency on the down-stroke. One might think that the bird hears the bell-buoy, so that the function of the bell is verified.

Alex Colville, "Remarks", November 1993

26.01

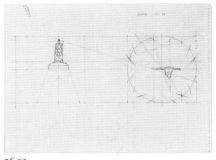

26.03

sion beginning with .3 and adding the previous number to the next, giving .6, .9, 1.5, 2.4, 3.9 and 6.3 – confirms that this is an application of the Fibonacci series. Combinations of various numbers further along in the progression yield the actual dimensions of the print in centimetres: 20.4 by 53.4. On 3 December, Colville did a drawing to the actual size of the print. On it, the distance of the horizon line up from the horizontal median is 2.4 cm, the same as the distance down from the median to the tip of the cormorant's flight feathers. The vertical lines framing the head and beak of the bird and the mass of its body are also 2.4 cm wide. The horizontal median is 10.2 cm from the framing edges, and the inscribed squares repeat the 20.4-cm height of the picture. The bell buoy is 12.6 cm from the left framing edge.

The cormorant and the bell buoy are caught in a net of eternal proportions and intervals. Concise, condensed images displaying not so much their own situation in the world as the essential condition of our being, they are present here, against the backdrop of a melancholy sea, as participants in all that is, yet condemned to be inevitably, ineluctably, alone.

26.02

26. BELL BUOY AND CORMORANT, 1985

Serigraph, 9/70
23.3 x 56.9 cm
Numbered, signed, dated
Courtesy of the Drabinsky Gallery, Toronto

The container ships which call at Halifax move majestically out to sea. They represent trade, activity; the recumbent man on the bench is inactive.

Alex Colville, "Remarks", November 1993

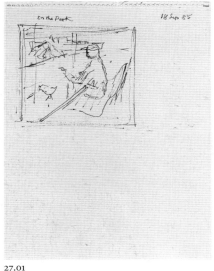

27.01

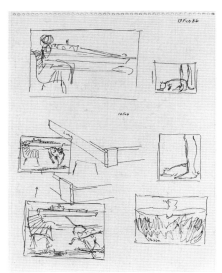

27.02

The sky is grey, sprinkled with a few light clouds. The day is chill. The surface of the harbour, calmly rippling an intense deep blue, is barely disturbed as a massive black and maroon freight boat, the *Köln Express,* passes from left to right through the middle plane of the picture, not far from the snow-banked shore in the foreground. The ship, laden with cargo containers, draws a narrow, flowing line of foam where it glides through the depths, perhaps on its way out to sea. A far shore or islands can be seen on the horizon, and to the right, on the edge where the waters meet the sky before disappearing to the other side of the world, two distant objects, possibly another boat or a house and a lighthouse, mark the critical division between what is here in the picture and what is out there, forever excluded from view. Standing in the foreground at an oblique angle to both the picture plane and the freighter, there is a wooden bench, one end projecting from the lower framing edge, the other meeting the horizontal median not far from the left framing edge. A man dressed in a warm grey winter coat, black boots and a fur hat lies stretched out the length of the bench on his back, his head to the lower right, his gloved hands folded on his stomach. The area of his face below the eyes can be seen in profile. Though the day is cold, it looks like he has fallen asleep.

The theme for *Köln Express* seems to have first occurred in sketches done while Colville was visiting Hong Kong in early 1985. These images show a "tourist", usually in the close foreground, with a freighter at various angles occupying a large portion of the middle ground. On 18 September of that year, a roughly square sketch annotated "In the Park" shows a figure seated on a bench angled from left to right; a bird walks in front of the bench on a sidewalk or a wharf and, in the distant middle ground, a freighter passes. On 13 and 14 February 1986, similar images appear on a page along with sketches for *Cat and Dog* as well as a visual note, perhaps for *Raven,* and what must be studies for the corner of a frame. In the uppermost of the pertinent images, the bench has been moved to the left and is positioned at right angles to the picture plane; the seated person faces right, and the ship passing in the middle ground also seems to be directed towards the right. In the two lower images, the bench and boat are still in about the same position, but in them, a dog with a stick in its mouth runs in front of the bench towards the viewer. There is nobody on the bench, which implies that the seated person is now playing with the dog and that this person might be the artist-viewer. By 24 February, the figure is once again present, now lying on the bench, which crosses the lower area of the picture at an angle, higher on the left than on the right. The dog is still included, but what it may be doing is less clear than before. By 27 February to 10 March, perspective and colour studies were well under way. Colours and their proposed uses are listed on a sheet from 7 March, with a drawing dated the 9th and 10th that shows the vanishing

27. KÖLN EXPRESS, 1986

Serigraph, 46/70
55.2 x 75.5 cm
Numbered, signed, dated
Mrs. P. Marko collection, courtesy of the Douglas Udell Gallery, Edmonton

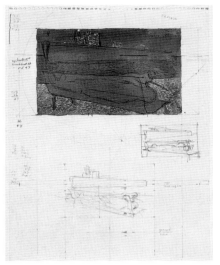

27.03

point; above a colour sketch dated the 10th and 12th, a note near some colour mixes gives the instructions "paper should be greyer – colder; red lighter – more neutral – print before green; brown slightly darker; make blue greener – darker; keep sky light – no d. grey; make d. grey warmer – y. ochre w r. umber". There are two colour photos most likely taken in early March. One is of an express freighter loaded with cargo containers; the other is of a park bench seen at an angle. The latter is taken from a position slightly more distant than that of the station point of the viewer of the print. A set-up Polaroid shows a view of the man (modelled by Colville) lying on a measured-off floor at the required angle, hands folded on stomach, wearing gloves, a winter coat and fur hat. Once satisfied with the adjustments made in the subsequent studies, Colville drew the image to the proposed measurements for the print on a sheet of coated translucent Mylar in preparation for the printing process.

Carrying its massive cargo, the freighter glides through the waters of the port, signifying either arrival or departure. Focussing attention on the transition between what is *here*, to be seen, and what is *there*, out of view, it catalyzes our sense of other distances, other absences – that of the man, who, though lying on the bench in our presence, has withdrawn inside himself to some private world of his own, inaccessible to us, and that suggested by the objects on the horizon, the immense elsewhere which, lying behind all the shapes we can now see, provides the background of our experience of the world.

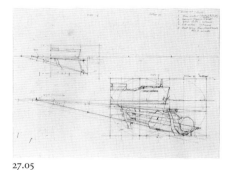

27.05

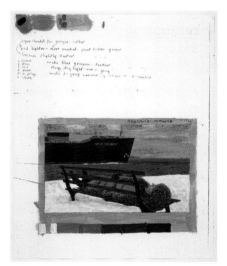

27.06

A wooden stairway rises from the right foreground of the image, pauses at the horizontal median as it extends into a landing which crosses almost the complete width of the picture, then rises once more through the upper left middle ground, stark, sharply delineated and profiled against the grey, cloud-strewn sky. The steps climb over boulders, of a retaining wall perhaps, or of a rocky shore, which are only slightly warmer in their brown hue than the cold grey of the wood. A dog with fur patterned in black, white and a warm yellow-brown, a dog with the radiant glow of gold, lies stretched out on the platform, parallel to the picture plane, head facing left, chewing on a bone. Though she is engaged in the serious business of gnawing, she keeps her eyes open, alert.

Rough sketches on a sheet of green paper dated 11 August 1987 show several approaches to the theme of *Le chien d'or*: the stairs are seen at different angles, there is a suggestion of rocky terrain, and the dog, though always parallel to the proposed picture planes, lies at various distances from them. From this point on, what seems to have preoccupied Colville is the exact relationship of the dog to the width, angle and rise of the stairway and the impact this had on the format of the image. By 13 and 15 August, the dog is lying centred on the horizontal median, with rocks piled in the middle ground to the right but with only a suggestion of the stairs to the left. On the 19th, the dog is still quite centrally positioned, but the rocks to the right have disappeared and the stairs climb behind the dog's head and shoulders to intersect the left side of the top framing edge. There follows some overlapping of solutions: in the same time span that the final arrangement appears – for example in the geometric drawing dated from 17 August to 5 September and the drawing with a verbal colour key of 24 August – there is also a detailed rendering in ink, acrylic and graphite pencil dated from 22 August to 10 September, which places the dog a bit to the left and shows only a narrow section of the stairs behind her muzzle. The solution finally adopted appears in studies of 27 August and 7 and 8 September, where differences can nevertheless be noticed in the number of risers in the stairs to the back and the amount of sky above.

Although interested in the bone, this dog has chosen her spot on the landing with care. She takes her job seriously, she never goes off duty. Holding the strategic position between the bottom and the top of the stairs, she is prepared for action in either direction. There are things to notice, people to look after, to play with, to protect. She is always ready. She is worth her weight in gold, this *chien d'or*.

I have admired the golden dog on the pediment of an old building in Quebec City near the Chateau Frontenac.
"I am a dog that gnaws a bone
In gnawing it I take my rest.
A time will come which is not yet
When I shall bite him who has
bitten me."
Someone I respect once said that I work like a dog chewing a bone; I consider this a compliment.

Alex Colville, "Remarks", November 1993

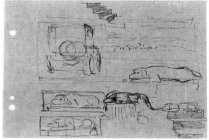

28.01

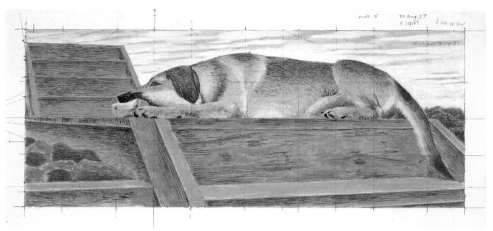

28.05

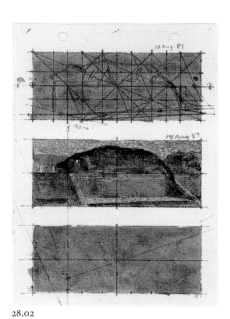

28.02

28.03

28. LE CHIEN D'OR, 1987

Serigraph, 39/70
Image: 26 x 62.8 cm
Numbered, signed, dated
Mrs. J. Guilbert collection, courtesy of the Douglas Udell Gallery, Edmonton

We acquired an AGA stove, which became a kind of centre of our life. In this serigraph my wife and our dog look into one of the ovens – a domestic scene.

Alex Colville, "Remarks", November 1993

The massive cast-iron Aga stove stands to the left of the picture at an oblique angle, its cobalt blue enamel finish and chrome hardware gleaming in the brightly lit kitchen, its base aligned with the brick red floor tiles. In the middle ground, to the right of the far end of the stove, a woman dressed in white holds the door to the upper oven open, bending down and forward at the hips to look inside. Her blond hair falls beside her turned head, hiding all her facial features except the tip of her nose. Her pose is contained, assured, elegant. Her left leg is advanced a bit to the front, knee bent slightly; her feet, in medium-heeled grey shoes, are at an angle to each other, providing stability to the leaning weight of her upper body. A circular metal bracelet hangs at her left wrist, confirming, as in *Woman on Diving Board*, the pull of gravity, and bright white light coming from the upper right, no doubt from a window outside the picture, sharply outlines the form of her back, bent hip and leg. She gently grips the stove handle. At ease, she is quite aware of what she is doing. Between the picture plane and the stove, only slightly out of line with the floor tiles, the household's mongrel, a "Shepherd X", stands with her rump towards the viewer, peering into the dark cavity of the open oven. Her face, like that of her mistress, is not visible, but we can see in her posture a relaxed inquisitiveness. Everything is going fine. The background is closed by a corner of the kitchen – to the right, a white wall, to the left, a closed door and a wood-panelled wall.

On 4 October 1988, Colville made two diagrams and a figure sketch that show basic information about the layout to be subsequently developed for *Stove*. What seems to be the earlier of the diagrams shows the ovens in two tiers, indicates eye level, and carries marginal measurements and notes that fix the viewer's station point (marked "s. p.") in respect to the "join of stove". The right edge of the stovepipe lines up with what would seem to be the "join", a vertical division drawn with a sketchy double line. Dated the same day, and 6 and 12 October as well, the other much more detailed diagram almost eliminates the closest set of ovens, placing the join much farther to the left of the picture. A note about measurements says that it is "51 cm from E. edge of vertical join to W. edge of oven opening and from that point 47 cm to E corner of stove", and to the side, accompanied with an arrow, we read that what must be the "join" is a "band 3 cm wide". The figure sketch of the woman and dog was done over a pale photocopy of the latter diagram and clearly indicates the line of sight, the station point in line with the join, the right-hand vanishing point and the position of the other vanishing point off the paper to the left. A more complete view of the arrangement is presented in a drawing on grey-green paper dated 6 and 12 October. The drawings from 2 to 12 November make extensive use of photocopying to work out the geometric configuration and the adjustments of the figures. Of particular interest is the appearance of the spiral, already

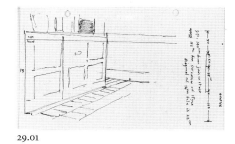

29.01

29. STOVE, 1988

Serigraph, 19/70
Image: 49.8 x 49.8 cm
Numbered, signed, dated
Dr E. Charleton collection, courtesy of the Douglas Udell Gallery, Vancouver

suggested by the geometric study on a page from 11 October, which draws the heads of the woman and the dog together and towards the open oven in one flowing movement of complicity.

The two mistresses of this home know what's cooking.

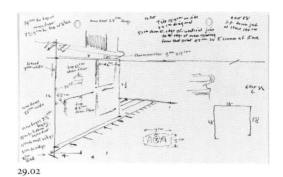

29.02

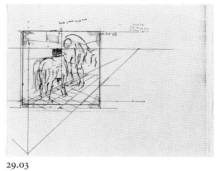

29.03

29.07

Swooping past the grassy slope where you pause, banking slightly as if to wheel into one of the rare updrafts on this heavy day, the dark shape of a raven looms, announcing itself in stark relief against the leaden grey sky. Its right wing is raised and the tips of its flight feathers are splayed, allowing air and light to pass between; its left wing, lower, cuts behind the contour of a slope. The great bird's body, heavier than that of its close relative the crow, slants slightly upward, parallel to the slope, its profiled beak curving downward and its tail forming the diamond fan characteristic of its species. Although the blackest of light-absorbent black, the bird's feathering can be seen outlined against the absence of colour, against this velvet-textured onyx, against this sudden void which resonates with the inevitable presence of fate. This is the consummate black of fullness, of what can hold no more; this the black of emptiness, of what is not and never shall be; this a black which declares its name: RAVEN. The word, heavy with premonition and complete in its closed symmetry, opens upward and outward from its centre, separating what comes before from what comes after. Now, as the raven passes, we might recall the unavoidable split, the mysterious space between life and death, and hear, as if in an echo, the darksome messenger quote with the poet: "Nevermore."

The theme of a broad-winged bird with a diamond-shaped tail soaring over grassy terrain occurs as early as 1984 in several formats, all horizontal rectangles, and a similar image appears on the matrix page of 13 and 14 February 1986, in conjunction with sketches for *Köln Express* and *Cat and Dog*. Four years later, during January and February 1990, the tentative format has become a vertical rectangle divided by the inscription of a circle within a square seated on a horizontal rectangle; the bird, winging from left to right, usually occupies a large proportion of the square, but the angle as well as the nature and proportion of the terrain over which it flies shift from image to image. One small sketch executed on 22 January shows the angle of the raven's wings at 14 degrees, its lower flight feathers extended below the contour of a hill, and the name "RAVEN" printed out in line with the edges of the image. In May of the same year, both horizontal and vertical rectangles were being considered in conjunction with variations in the angle of the bird's flight, the position of the bird's wings and the composition of the landscape. The solution, which harks back to the sketch of 22 January with the bird's wings set at 14 degrees off the vertical, appears on 16 May in a drawing on green paper which barely suggests the position of the wings relative to the terrain. The angle of the bird is taken up again in reworked drawings with final dates of 11 and 20 June in which the geometric structure is evident and the landscape becomes the edge of a grassy hill.

I see ravens frequently; they are very big and powerful. This one flies over a dyke, which is built to hold back the tide.
Alex Colville, "Remarks", November 1993

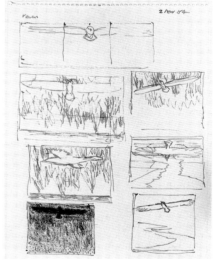

30.01

Although its apparition is a purely imaginary construct, the ebony bird flashes into our field of vision, focussing in the ambiguous density of its soaring image an awareness of what is ultimately left to us as real – our fleeting presence in the world.

30.05

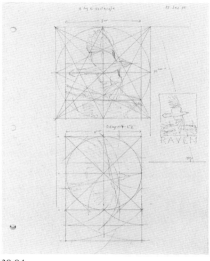

30.04

30.07

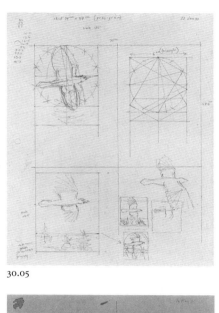

30.12

R A V E N

30. RAVEN, 1990

Serigraph, 27/70
81.1 x 53.8 cm
Numbered, signed, dated
Courtesy of the Drabinsky Gallery, Toronto

An example of stunt-flying by a non-human. I have never seen this, but a raven would certainly be capable of this feat.

Alex Colville, "Remarks", November 1993

Swooping under the bridge and about to emerge into the open, the raven appears as a swift darkness in the shadows, opening its beak in a raucous cry of anticipated triumph. The imaged sound, a guttural "crouwak-crouwak", reverberates in the confined space below the iron span under which you, ducking your head instinctively, are about pass. You know this bridge. It is the same construction that, during a winter drive, was profiled in the snowy landscape, a sign of transition, a background for your choice as a *Traveller*, and the same structure on which you saw, in the warmer light of summer, the curious asymmetrical union of the mature *Couple on Bridge*. Now the bridge, about to pass above you as you move on below, becomes the stable axis in a crossing of ways punctuated by the swift, vibrant presence of the raven. Though conveying permanence through the solidity of its mottled concrete pile and iron beams, the bridge, considered from above, is a place of conveyance, of transition, and from below, a place of passage. With both points of view taken together, the bridge is an intersection, a place of change. Here, laden with the crafty knowledge and wisdom of its species, the raven erupts into view, announcing as it has from time immemorial the perplexing but inevitable task of humankind: to achieve freedom by choosing fate.

This print is displayed alone, without accompanying sketches or drawings.

31. BRIDGE AND RAVEN, 1993

Serigraph, 16/70
37 x 56.2 cm
Numbered, signed, dated
Courtesy of the Drabinsky Gallery, Toronto

Flying is more interesting than shaving.

Alex Colville, "Remarks", November 1993

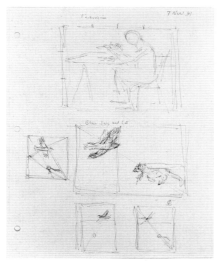

32.01

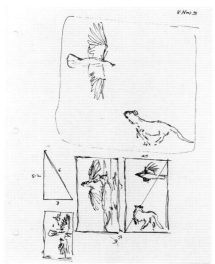

32.02

A maroon-red memory of last night's deep shades still pervades the room as the artist, electric razor in his left hand, repeats once again his ritual daily shave. Chin raised, neck pulled slightly to the side, he passes the humming blades along the taut skin covering the left side of his jaw, once again undoing what nature has wrought, once again submitting to curious human standards of propriety and style. The face should appear clean, fresh, unencumbered by obvious traces of the spontaneous animal life of the body. A predisposition of mind, the imperious rule of culture, directs this operation, and it proceeds as always with resignation and an absent stare at the ceiling. Standing so close to the picture plane that his torso is cropped just below the shoulders, the artist is back-lit by the brightness of a new day shining through a window off centre to the right in the advanced middle ground. Outside, a Blue Jay flies past, busy doing one of the uncharacteristically silent early morning errands proper to its species. Lost in his ritual, the artist misses seeing the splendid blue flash by the window. The jay doesn't care.

Before its appearance in the artist's window, the Blue Jay image was the subject of sketches and studies for what could have – and still might – become quite different works. Over the years, Colville has drawn rapid visual notations of birds in flight, sometimes so general in delineation that it is difficult to determine with certitude which species was the object of his concern. One such drawing, for example, shows a bird winging from the top right-hand corner of the image towards another bird seated on a fence or gatepost with trees and perhaps houses in the background. Above the image the words "Blue Jays" are inscribed. Later, the theme shifts with the introduction of a cat. A matrix page of 7 November 1991 shows four variants of the bird being watched by the cat, one in a horizontal rectangle above which is written "Blue Jay and Cat", the other three in diverse vertical formats. Of note is another sketch on the same page entitled "Technician", which shows a human figure at a drawing board, working on what might be a bird image. Further elaborations focus on the cat, either on the ground or climbing a tree, but always watching the bird with some degree of surprise or fascination. By December 1991 and January 1992, the artist was executing ink and acrylic drawings in which the jay flies either from right to left or left to right past the cat, which hugs a tree trunk on either the left or right. The relative scales and positions of the bird, tree trunk and cat also change from drawing to drawing. To date, the relationship developed in the "Blue Jay and Cat" image has not been used directly for a painting or a print but lies, not entirely dormant, as a latent interpretative dimension of *Artist and Blue Jay,* especially when it is considered in conjunction with the "Technician" sketch. The cat, undistracted by the requirements of culture, has a keener, more immediate awareness than the artist with his razor.

32. ARTIST AND BLUE JAY, 1993

Serigraph, 8/70
38.2 x 55.8 cm
Numbered, signed, dated
Courtesy of the Drabinsky Gallery, Toronto

32.06

32.07

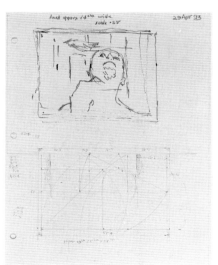

32.08

By late April 1993, the artist-technician was no longer at the drawing board and had become involved in both climbing the ladder of the wharf seen in *Arrival* and shaving in front of an open window. A matrix page dated 29 April shows several of these views, notably a close-up sketch in a round format on a wash background of the artist shaving with his right hand and an image in a rectangular format showing the artist in dark silhouette, perhaps facing the window through which a bird flying from right to left can be seen. On another page dated the same day, there is a sketch in which the artist, shaving with his right hand, faces the picture plane; the bird, still flying from right to left, is tentatively positioned in the window roughly delineated behind him. Below this image there is a geometric study with measurements that places the artist's head right of centre. Further drawings from 30 April to 5 and 6 May elaborate the image and its underlying geometry in coloured ink and acrylic paint. At some point during this period, a Polaroid photo taken on 29 April was printed on transparent Mylar and reversed, placing the artist's head to the left of centre and showing him shaving with his left hand. The reversed position, with the jay flying from left to right, occurs in a signed drawing accompanied by colour samples and colour notes dated 12 and 13 May. Geometric studies made on the same and subsequent days using a circle and a spiral deal with both the original and reversed positions, but as is shown by the geometric studies of later May and early June and a full-size drawing dated 16 and 17 May, it is the reversed position that was finally chosen.

Artist and Blue Jay, in the manner of Colville's other works involving mammals and birds, draws attention to troubling things deeply embedded in current attitudes and processes. Ours is a culture of amnesia, so preoccupied with the perfection of its own structure that it is forgetful of its real lifeblood, its continued dependency on the nonhuman world for its substance, for its energy, for its ability to inspire wonder. Like the artist absent-mindedly engrossed in the repetition of a ritual, it is we who lose something if we cannot liberate our minds enough to be astonished by the Blue Jay.

On request, the artist has saved unsatisfactory proofs from each of the five printing runs to show the sequenced layering of the colours: medium-tone black with yellow ochre, dark red, white, blue and black. These are inscribed with the words "spoil proof", the number and colour of the run, and in some cases, a comment.

The exhibition ends by returning the viewer to the entrance where the two Colville paintings in the collection of the Montreal Museum of Fine Arts hang. The horse still thunders forward on its swift, silent hooves towards the open churchyard gate, and the crow still flies, forever suspended over the field of ripening barley. Nothing in the images has changed. But for us, there is the newness of the instant in which we perceive...

Exit

Crows do not always fly in a straight line. Sometimes, even as they go about their daily tasks, they delight in play, launching themselves with a downward glide on their great wings from the bare branches of seasonal change, skimming low for a moment as if to barely caress the ground; then, swooping upward, higher and higher into the resplendent air, they wheel, bank, cavort, their ebony shapes making, as my friend Trevor Smith recently remarked, "black holes in the sky". If we permit ourselves to wonder as we watch, we can take wing with the crows, the threads of their dark aerial pattern resonating with the mystery of our presence, of our inexorable flight from a past held only by memory into a future which, like those black holes in the sky, is full of absence and hope.

List of exhibited works

The Paintings

A. CYCLIST AND CROW, 1981
B. CHURCH AND HORSE, 1964
1. ARRIVAL, 1991
2. LOOKING DOWN, 1988
3. BOAT AND BATHER, 1984
4. LOW TIDE, 1987
5. FLOATING WOMAN, 1990
6. WOMAN ON DIVING BOARD, 1989
7. WHITE CANOE, 1987
8. VERANDAH, 1983
9. COUPLE ON BRIDGE, 1992
10. TARGET SHOOTING, 1990
11. WOMAN WITH REVOLVER, 1987
12. CAT AND DOG, 1986
13. DOG AND GROOM, 1991
14. BAT, 1989
15. SINGER, 1986
16. HORSE AND GIRL, 1984
17. FRENCH CROSS, 1988
18. CHAPLAIN, 1991
19. WESTERN STAR, 1985
20. TAXI, 1985
21. TRAVELLER, 1992
0. KISS WITH HONDA, 1989 (not exhibited)
22. SWIMMER AND SUN, 1993

The Serigraphs

23. KINGFISHER, 1983
24. RAT, 1983
25. FÊTE CHAMPÊTRE, 1984
26. BELL BUOY AND CORMORANT, 1985
27. KÖLN EXPRESS, 1986
28. LE CHIEN D'OR, 1987
29. STOVE, 1988
30. RAVEN, 1990
31. BRIDGE AND RAVEN, 1993
32. ARTIST AND BLUE JAY, 1993

The Drawings

CYCLIST AND CROW

A.01 *03/07/1981*
Raw sienna and black ink on white paper, 22.8 x 30.4 cm
Collection of the artist

A.02 *04/07/1981*
Raw sienna and sepia ink on white paper, 22.8 x 30.6 cm
Collection of the artist

A.03 *10,13,14,16/07/1981*
Raw sienna, maroon and black ink on paper, 30.4 x 22.8 cm
Collection of the artist

CHURCH AND HORSE

B.01 *27/12/1963*
Raw sienna ink and graphite on white paper, 27.4 x 34.7 cm
Collection of the artist

B.02 *28,30/12/1963*
Red and black ink and graphite on white paper, 27.3 x 34.4 cm
Collection of the artist

B.03 *30/12/1963*
Raw sienna, red and black ink and graphite on white paper, 34.5 x 27.3 cm
Collection of the artist

B.04 *02/01/1964*
Raw sienna and black ink on white paper, 27.3 x 34.5 cm
Collection of the artist

B.05 *02,03,04/01/1964*
Red and black ink and graphite on white paper, 34.7 x 27.3 cm
Collection of the artist

B.06 *04,06,07,08,09/01/1964*
Red and yellow ink and graphite on white paper, 48.2 x 91.4 (3 unequal flaps attached from behind with masking tape)
Collection of the artist

B.07 *06/01/1964*
Graphite on letterhead, 27.9 x 21.5 cm
Collection of the artist

B.08 *24,27,29/01/1964 and 04/02/1964*
Red and yellow ink and graphite on white paper, 42.6 x 35.5 cm
Collection of the artist

ARRIVAL

1.01 *26/07/1991*
Sepia ink on white paper, 28 x 21.7 cm
Collection of the artist

1.02 *27/07/1991*
Sepia ink on white paper, 28 x 21.7 cm
Collection of the artist

1.03 *10/08/1991*
Sepia ink on white paper, 28 x 21.7 cm
Collection of the artist

1.04 *05/09/1991 (a)*
(Nos. 1 and 2 in series)
Raw sienna ink on white paper, 28 x 21.7 cm
Collection of the artist

1.05 *05/09/1991 (b)*
(No. 3 in series)
Raw sienna ink on white paper, 28 x 21.7 cm
Collection of the artist

1.06 *11/09/1991*
Raw sienna and orange ink and wash on white paper, 28 x 21.7 cm
Collection of the artist

1.07 *13/09/1991*
Orange, blue and black ink on white paper, 28 x 21.7 cm
Collection of the artist

1.08 *24/09/1991*
Raw sienna, sepia and orange ink and grey wash on white paper, 21.7 x 28 cm
Collection of the artist

1.09 *26/09/1991*
Orange and blue ink and acrylic on green paper, 27.5 x 21.6 cm
Collection of the artist

1.10 *29,30/09/1991*
Orange, grey and black ink on green paper, 21.6 x 27.5 cm
Collection of the artist

LOOKING DOWN

2.01 *23/01/1988*
Raw sienna ink on white card, 13.9 x 21.5 cm
Collection of the artist

2.02 *17/02/1988*
Raw sienna ink on white paper, 28 x 21.6 cm
Collection of the artist

2.03 *20/02/1988*
Raw sienna ink on white paper, 28 x 21.6 cm
Collection of the artist

2.04 *01/03/1988*
Raw sienna and black ink on photo-copy on white paper, 21.7 x 27.9 cm
Collection of the artist

2.05 *08,21,23/03/1988*
Raw sienna and blue ink on white paper, 21.6 x 28 cm
Collection of the artist

2.06 *08,09/03/1988*
Acrylic on paper, 21.6 x 28 cm
Collection of the artist

2.07 *15/05/1988*
Black ink and graphite on white card, 14 x 21.6 cm
Collection of the artist

2.08 *25,26,28/03/1988*
Raw sienna and white ink and wash on white paper, 21.6 x 28 cm
Collection of the artist

BOAT AND BATHER

3.01 *No date*
Raw sienna and blue ink and graphite on photocopy on white paper, 27.9 x 21.6 cm
Collection of the artist

3.02 *19,20/07/1984*
Raw sienna ink and watercolour on white paper, 30.4 x 22.8 cm
Collection of the artist

3.03 *20/07/1984*
Raw sienna, orange and blue ink on white paper, 30.4 x 22.8 cm
Collection of the artist

3.04 *20/07/1984*
Yellow wax crayon and brown wash on white paper, 30.4 x 22.8 cm
Collection of the artist

3.05 *24/07/1984*
Raw sienna and blue ink, white wax crayon and brown wash on white paper, 30.3 x 22.8 cm
Collection of the artist

3.06 *25/07/1984 to 02/08/1984*
Raw sienna and blue ink and graphite on white paper, 29 x 22.8 cm
Collection of the artist

3.07 *12/08/1984 (a)*
Sepia ink on white paper, 20.1 x 13.4 cm
Collection of the artist

3.08 *12/08/1984 (b)*
Sepia ink on white paper, 13.4 x 20.1 cm
Collection of the artist

3.09 *13/08/1984*
Sepia ink on white paper, 20.1 x 13.4 cm
Collection of the artist

3.10 *14/08/1984 to 20/08/1984*
Raw sienna ink and graphite on white paper, 28.9 x 22.8 cm
Collection of the artist

3.11 *23/08/1984*
Sepia ink on white paper, 20.1 x 13.4 cm
Collection of the artist

LOW TIDE

4.01 *03/11/1986*
Raw sienna, orange, blue and grey ink and graphite on white paper, 29.8 x 22.4 cm
Collection of the artist

4.02 *03/11/1986*
Raw sienna ink on white paper, 29.7 x 22 cm
Collection of the artist

4.03 *05/11/1986*
Raw sienna, orange and grey ink on white paper, 22.1 x 29.6 cm
Collection of the artist

4.04 *06,07/11/1986*
Raw sienna, orange, blue, white and grey ink on grey-green paper, 29.8 x 21.8 cm
Collection of the artist

4.05 *15/12/1986*
Black ink on white paper, 22 x 29.6 cm
Collection of the artist

4.06 *16/12/1986 (Mylar) and 11,12/01/1987 (paper)*
Blue and black ink on Mylar, raw sienna ink and graphite on white paper, Mylar: 12 x 21 cm; paper: 18 x 26.5 cm
Collection of the artist

4.07 *10,11,12/12/1986*
Raw sienna, blue and white ink on grey-green paper, 30.1 x 21.8 cm
Collection of the artist

4.08 *14,17/11/1986*
Raw sienna, white and grey ink on grey-green paper, 28 x 21.6 cm
Mr. R. Fraser Elliott collection

4.09 *15/12/1986*
Raw sienna and grey ink, acrylic and graphite on white paper, 28.1 x 22 cm
Mr. R. Fraser Elliott collection

FLOATING WOMAN

5.01 *23/08/1990*
Raw sienna, blue and black ink on white paper, 28 x 21.6 cm
Collection of the artist

5.02 *24/08/1990*
Raw sienna, orange, blue and black ink on grey-green paper, 27.6 x 21.4 cm
Collection of the artist

5.03 *05/10/1990*
Raw sienna, orange and blue ink on white paper, 28 x 21.6 cm
Collection of the artist

5.04 *09/10/1990 (a)*
Black ink on white card, 14.4 x 20.4 cm
Collection of the artist

5.05 *09/10/1990 (b)*
Black ink on white card, 14.4 x 20.4 cm
Collection of the artist

5.06 *09/10/1990 (c)*
Black ink on white card, 14.4 x 20.4 cm
Collection of the artist

5.07 *09,18/10/90 and 04,05/11/90*
Black and white ink, graphite and grey wash on photocopy on white paper, 21.6 x 28 cm
Collection of the artist

WOMAN ON DIVING BOARD

6.01 *10/05/1989*
Raw sienna, white and grey ink on grey-green paper, 21.6 x 27.6 cm
Private collection

6.02 *16,17/04/1989*
Raw sienna, blue and black ink and graphite on grey-green paper, 21.8 x 27.6 cm
Collection of the artist, courtesy of the Drabinsky Gallery, Toronto

6.03 *21/04/1989*
Black ink on white paper, 12.8 x 20.3 cm
Collection of the artist

6.04 *24/04/1989*
Blue ink, graphite and fax toner on fax paper, 21.7 x 29 cm
Collection of the artist, courtesy of the Drabinsky Gallery, Toronto

6.05 *24,25/04/1989*
Blue ink, graphite and fax toner on fax paper, 21.7 x 29 cm
Collection of the artist, courtesy of the Drabinsky Gallery, Toronto

6.06 *10/05/1989*
Blue ink, graphite and fax toner on fax paper, 21.7 x 29 cm
Collection of the artist, courtesy of the Drabinsky Gallery, Toronto

WHITE CANOE

7.01 *23/04/1987 (a)*
Black ink on white paper, 11.2 x 15.2 cm
Collection of the artist

7.02 *23/04/1987 (b)*
Raw sienna and blue ink on white paper, 29.6 x 22 cm
Collection of the artist

7.03 *29/04/1987 and 01/05/1987*
Ink and acrylic on white paper, 29.7 x 21.5 cm
Collection of the artist

7.04 *06/05/1987 to 01/06/1987*
Raw sienna, blue and black ink and graphite on white paper, 28.4 x 23.4 cm
Collection of the artist

7.05 *25/05/1987 to 01/06/1987*
Raw sienna, blue and white ink and grey-brown wash on white paper, 29.7 x 21.5 cm
Collection of the artist

VERANDAH

8.01 *30/05/1983*
Sepia ink on white paper, 30.5 x 22.9 cm
Collection of the artist, courtesy of the Drabinsky Gallery, Toronto

8.02 *01/06/1983*
Raw sienna ink on white paper, 30.4 x 22.8 cm
Collection of the artist

8.03 *01,02/06/1983*
Raw sienna ink on white paper, 30.4 x 22.8 cm
Collection of the artist

8.04 *15/06/1983*
Raw sienna ink and graphite on white paper, 22.8 x 30.4 cm
Collection of the artist

8.05 *15/06/1983 to 24/06/1983*
Raw sienna and black ink and graphite on tracing paper, 18.2 x 18 cm
Collection of the artist

8.06 *15,16,17/06/1983*
Orange ink and graphite on white paper, 26.4 x 39.1 cm
Collection of the artist, courtesy of the Drabinsky Gallery, Toronto

8.07 *28/01/1983*
Brown and black ink, graphite and colour photograph on paper, photograph: 8.4 x 12.5 cm; paper: 24.1 x 12.5 cm
Collection of the artist, courtesy of the Drabinsky Gallery, Toronto

8.08 *02,03,04,05,12/08/1983*
Ink and graphite on white paper, 26.2 x 31.2 cm
Collection of the artist, courtesy of the Drabinsky Gallery, Toronto

8.09 *12/08/1983 (Mylar) and 05,12/08/1983 (paper)*
Raw sienna, maroon and black ink and graphite on white paper, with Mylar overlay, 21.5 x 27.8 cm
Collection of the artist

COUPLE ON BRIDGE

9.01 *01/06/1992*
Raw sienna ink on white paper, 28 x 21.7 cm
Collection of the artist

9.02 *02/06/1992*
Raw sienna ink on white paper, 28 x 21.7 cm
Collection of the artist

9.03 *02/06/1992*
Raw sienna ink on white paper, 28 x 21.7 cm
Collection of the artist

9.04 *07/06/1992 (a)*
(No. 1 in series)
Sepia, orange and black ink on translucent coated Mylar, 21.7 x 13.9 cm
Collection of the artist

9.05 *07/06/1992 (b)*
(No. 2 in series)
Sepia, orange and black ink on translucent coated Mylar, 14 x 21.7 cm
Collection of the artist

9.06 *07/06/1992 (c)*
(No. 3 in series)
Sepia and orange ink on translucent coated Mylar, 14.1 x 21.7 cm
Collection of the artist

9.07 *03,04/07/1992*
Acrylic on photocopy on white paper, 27.7 x 21.5 cm
Collection of the artist

9.08 *17,18/07/1992*
Raw sienna, orange and black ink and grey-green wash on heavy white paper, 28.3 x 21.5 cm
Collection of the artist

9.09 *[?]/07/1992*
Raw sienna, blue and grey ink and grey wash on heavy white paper, 28.1 x 21.8 cm
Collection of the artist

9.10 *07/07/1992*
Acrylic on paper, 28 x 21.5 cm
Collection of the artist, courtesy of the Drabinsky Gallery, Toronto

9.11 *12,18,27/06/1992*
Red, white and black ink on grey paper, 22.1 x 27.8 cm
Collection of the artist

9.12 *18/01/1993 (didactic drawing)*
Raw sienna and black ink and graphite on white paper, 28 x 21.6 cm
Collection of the artist, courtesy of the Drabinsky Gallery, Toronto

TARGET SHOOTING

10.01 *19,30/12/1989 and 01/01/1990*
Raw sienna and grey ink on grey-green paper, 28.7 x 21.7 cm
Private collection

10.02 *14/11/1989*
Raw sienna and blue ink, wax crayon and wash on white paper, 27.9 x 21.5 cm
Collection of the artist

10.03 *17/11/1989 and 16/12/89*
Raw sienna and black ink on white paper, 27.9 x 21.5 cm
Collection of the artist

10.04 *18/12/1989*
Black ink on white paper, 20.3 x 12.7 cm
Collection of the artist

10.05 *29/12/1989*
Raw sienna ink on white paper, 27.9 x 21.5 cm
Collection of the artist

10.06 *No date*
Black ink on white paper, 20.3 x 12.7 cm
Collection of the artist

10.07 *15,16,22/12/1989*
Raw sienna ink on white paper, 28 x 21.6 cm
Collection of the artist, courtesy of the Drabinsky Gallery, Toronto

WOMAN WITH REVOLVER

11.01 *27/02/1986 (a)*
Raw sienna and white ink and black wash on white paper, 15 x 22.8 cm
Collection of the artist

11.02 *27/02/1986 (b)*
Raw sienna ink and grey wash on white paper, 14.8 x 22.8 cm
Collection of the artist

11.03 *27/02/1986 (c) (No. 2)*
Raw sienna ink on white paper, 15 x 22.8 cm
Collection of the artist

11.04 *02/04/1987*
Raw sienna, orange, grey and black ink and wax crayon on white paper, 29.9 x 22.3 cm
Collection of the artist

11.05 *06,07/04/1987*
Raw sienna, white and black ink on photocopy on grey-green paper, 22 x 30 cm
Collection of the artist

11.06 *10/04/1987*
Raw sienna, white and black ink on white paper, 22.2 x 29.3 cm
Collection of the artist

11.07 *27/11/1986*
Raw sienna, blue, white and black ink on grey-green paper, 21.7 x 30 cm
Collection of the artist

11.08 *24,25/11/1987*
Raw sienna, blue and grey ink on white paper, 21.7 x 28 cm
Collection of the artist

11.09 *05,07/12/1986*
Raw sienna, orange, blue, white and black ink on photocopy on grey-green paper, 14.1 x 19.7 cm
Collection of the artist

11.10 *20/12/1986*
Raw sienna ink on white paper, 29.8 x 22 cm
Collection of the artist

11.11 *21/12/1987*
Raw sienna, blue, white, grey and black ink on grey-green paper, 20.3 x 14.9 cm
Collection of the artist

CAT AND DOG

12.01 *21,28/03/1985*
Raw sienna and black ink and wash on white paper, 30.5 x 22.8 cm
Collection of the artist

12.02 *25/10/1985*
Raw sienna ink on white paper, 30.5 x 22.8 cm
Collection of the artist

12.03 *02,03,04/1986*
Raw sienna, white and black ink and wash on white paper, 14.8 x 22.5 cm
Collection of the artist

12.04 *04,07,09,10/04/1986*
Raw sienna, orange, white and black ink and graphite on brown paper, 30.5 x 22.8 cm
Collection of the artist

12.05 *10,11,13/04/1986*
Acrylic on card, 16 x 22.1 cm
Collection of the artist

DOG AND GROOM

13.01 *30/09/1990 (a)*
Raw sienna, blue and black ink and grey-blue wash on white paper, 28 x 21.6 cm
Collection of the artist

13.02 *30/09/1990 (b)*
Raw sienna ink on white paper, 28 x 21.6 cm
Collection of the artist

13.03 *02/10/1990*
Raw sienna, orange, blue, white and black ink on grey-green paper, 21.5 x 27.5 cm
Collection of the artist

13.04 *04/10/1990*
Raw sienna, orange and maroon ink on white paper, 28 x 21.6 cm
Collection of the artist

13.05 *10/10/1990*
Raw sienna ink on white paper, 28 x 21.6 cm
Collection of the artist

13.06 *23,25/10/1990*
Raw sienna, orange and blue ink on white paper, 28 x 21.6 cm
Collection of the artist

13.07 *12/12/1990*
Raw sienna ink on white paper, 28 x 21.6 cm
Collection of the artist

13.08 *20,22/12/1990*
Raw sienna, orange, maroon and white ink and grey wash on white paper, 28 x 21.6 cm
Collection of the artist

13.09 *03,04/01/1991*
Raw sienna and orange ink and acrylic on white paper, 28 x 21.7 cm
Collection of the artist

13.10 *07/01/1991*
Sepia and orange ink and acrylic on white paper, 21.7 x 28 cm
Collection of the artist

13.11 *08/01/1991*
Blue and maroon ink on photocopy
on white paper, 27.9 x 21.6 cm
Collection of the artist

13.12 *08/01/1991*
Blue ink on photocopy on white
paper, 27.9 x 21.6 cm
Collection of the artist

13.13 *06/02/1991 (paper) and
07,14/02/1991 (Mylar)*
Raw sienna, brown and orange ink
and graphite on white paper, with
Mylar overlay,
Mylar: 25.9 x 19.9 cm;
paper: 28 x 21.6 cm
Collection of the artist

BAT

14.01 *08/02/1989*
Raw sienna ink on white paper,
28 x 21.6 cm
Collection of the artist, courtesy of
the Drabinsky Gallery, Toronto

14.02 *10/02/1989*
Black ink on white paper,
28 x 21.6 cm
Collection of the artist, courtesy of
the Drabinsky Gallery, Toronto

14.03 *12/02/1989*
Raw sienna ink and grey wash on
white paper, 28 x 21.6 cm
Collection of the artist, courtesy of
the Drabinsky Gallery, Toronto

14.04 *14/02/1989*
Raw sienna and black ink and grey
wash on paper, 28 x 21.6 cm
Collection of the artist, courtesy of
the Drabinsky Gallery, Toronto

14.05 *12,13,14,15/02/1989*
Raw sienna, blue and white ink on
grey-green paper, 20.2 x 32.3 cm
Collection of the artist, courtesy of
the Drabinsky Gallery, Toronto

SINGER

15.01 *18/11/1985 (a)*
Raw sienna, orange and white ink
and sepia wash on white paper,
30.3 x 22.7 cm
Collection of the artist

15.02 *18/11/1985 (b)*
Raw sienna ink on white paper,
30.4 x 22.7 cm
Collection of the artist

15.03 *21,22/11/1985*
Raw sienna, orange and blue ink
and graphite on white paper,
30.4 x 22.8 cm
Collection of the artist

15.04 *22,23/12/1985*
Raw sienna and blue ink and
graphite on white paper,
30.4 x 22.8 cm
Collection of the artist

15.05 *03/12/1985*
Raw sienna, blue and black ink,
graphite and wash on white paper,
30.4 x 22.8 cm
Collection of the artist

15.06 *04,09/12/1985*
Raw sienna, white and black ink
and graphite on blue paper,
15.1 x 22.7 cm
Collection of the artist

15.07 *12,15/12/1985*
Raw sienna, blue and black ink and
graphite on brown paper,
22.7 x 30.5 cm
Collection of the artist

15.08 *20,21/12/1985*
Raw sienna, orange, blue, white and
black ink on yellow paper,
30.3 x 22.8 cm
Collection of the artist

15.09 *02,06/01/1986*
Raw sienna, blue, white and black
ink and graphite on brown paper,
22.8 x 30.5 cm
Collection of the artist

15.10 *02,06,07,09/01/1986*
Raw sienna, orange, blue and black
ink, graphite and white wax crayon
on off-white paper, 22.8 x 30.4 cm
Collection of the artist

15.11 *04/01/1986 (a)*
(No. 1 in series)
Blue ink on Polaroid with Mylar
overlay, 10.7 x 8.8 cm
Collection of the artist

15.12 *04/01/1986 (b)*
(No. 2 in series)
Blue ink on Polaroid with Mylar
overlay, 10.7 x 8.8 cm
Collection of the artist

15.13 *04/01/1986 (c)*
(No. 3 in series)
Blue ink on Polaroid with Mylar
overlay, 10.7 x 8.8 cm
Collection of the artist

15.14 *05/01/1986*
Polaroid, 10.7 x 8.8 cm
Collection of the artist

15.15 *No date*
Polaroid, 10.7 x 8.8 cm
Collection of the artist

15.16 *31/12/1985*
Wash on white paper,
image: 10 x 12 cm
Collection of the artist, courtesy of
the Drabinsky Gallery, Toronto

15.17 *20/12/1985*
Sepia and black ink over photocopy
of Polaroid, on white paper,
27.9 x 21.6 cm
Collection of the artist

15.18 *No date*
Polaroid with Mylar overlay,
10.7 x 8.8 cm
Collection of the artist

15.19 *No date*
Polaroid with Mylar overlay,
10.8 x 8.9
Collection of the artist

15.20 *No date*
Raw sienna and blue ink on colour
photograph, with Mylar overlay,
12.7 x 8.8 cm
Collection of the artist

HORSE AND GIRL

16.01 *14/11/1983*
Raw sienna ink on white paper,
30.4 x 22.8 cm
Collection of the artist

16.02 *16/11/1983*
Raw sienna and black ink over photocopy of photograph, on white
paper, 27.9 x 21.6 cm
Collection of the artist

16.03 *18/11/1983*
Raw sienna and black ink, white
wax crayon and wash on white
paper, 30.4 x 22.8 cm
Collection of the artist

16.04 *22,23/11/1983*
Raw sienna ink and graphite on
white paper, 30.3 x 22.8 cm
Collection of the artist

16.05 *23/11/1983*
Raw sienna and black ink, white,
pale blue and yellow wax crayon
and wash on white paper,
30.4 x 22.8 cm
Collection of the artist

16.06 *25/11/1983 to 01/12/1983*
Raw sienna ink and acrylic on white
cardboard, 27 x 24.2 cm
Collection of the artist

16.07 *29/11/1983*
Raw sienna, blue and black ink and
graphite on photocopy on white
paper, 27.9 x 21.5 cm
Collection of the artist

FRENCH CROSS

17.01 *10/09/1983*
Dark brown ink on white paper,
30.4 x 22.8 cm
Collection of the artist

17.02 *13/09/1983*
Maroon and black ink on white
paper, 30.4 x 22.8 cm
Collection of the artist

17.03 *27/10/1986*
Raw sienna and black ink, wax
crayon and wash on white paper,
22.2 x 29.7 cm
Collection of the artist

17.04 *23/07/1988*
Raw sienna and yellow ink on white
paper, 28 x 21.6 cm
Collection of the artist

17.05 *23/07/1988*
Yellow and green ink on white
paper, 27.9 x 21.6 cm
Collection of the artist

17.06 *24/07/1988*
Raw sienna and green ink on white
paper, 27.9 x 21.6 cm
Collection of the artist

17.07 *27/07/1988*
Green and black ink on white
paper, 27.7 x 21.6 cm
Collection of the artist

17.08 *24/07/1988*
Green ink and wash on white paper,
28 x 21.6 cm
Collection of the artist

17.09 *27/07/1988*
Polaroid, 13 x 12 cm
Collection of the artist

17.10 *11/07/1988*
Raw sienna and black ink on white
paper, 27 x 21.5 cm
Collection of the artist, courtesy of
the Drabinsky Gallery, Toronto

17.11 *30,31/07/1988*
Green ink on white paper,
27.5 x 21.5 cm
Collection of the artist, courtesy of
the Drabinsky Gallery, Toronto

17.12 *01/08/1988*
Red, green and blue ink on white
paper, 21.6 x 28 cm
Collection of the artist

17.13 *25,26/07/1988 and 08/08/1988*
Acrylic on photocopy on white
paper, image: 14 x 20 cm
Collection of the artist, courtesy of
the Drabinsky Gallery, Toronto

CHAPLAIN

18.01 *25/04/1991*
Black ink on heavy white paper,
20.3 x 14.3 cm
Collection of the artist

18.02 *08/05/1991*
Sepia ink on white paper,
14.3 x 20.4 cm
Collection of the artist

18.03 *16,17,21/05/1991 and*
03/06/1991
Raw sienna, orange, blue and black
ink on photocopy on white paper,
21.7 x 28 cm
Collection of the artist

18.04 *17,21/05/1991*
Raw sienna and black ink on white
paper, 20.4 x 14.5 cm
Collection of the artist

18.05 *18,21/05/1991*
Raw sienna, orange, blue and black
ink and graphite on grey-green
paper, 21.6 x 27.6 cm
Collection of the artist

18.06 *21/05/1991 (a)*
Black ink on white paper,
20.4 x 14.5 cm
Collection of the artist

18.07 *21/05/1991 (b)*
Black ink on white paper,
20.4 x 14.5 cm
Collection of the artist

18.08 *22,31/05/1991 and*
03,04,13/06/1991
Raw sienna, orange, blue and black
ink and graphite on white paper,
21.6 x 28 cm
Collection of the artist

18.09 *10/05/1991*
Raw sienna ink on photocopy on
white paper, 28 x 21.7 cm
Collection of the artist

18.10 *18/05/1991 and 01/06/91*
White and black ink on photocopy
on grey-green paper, 21.8 x 27.3 cm
Collection of the artist, courtesy of
the Drabinsky Gallery, Toronto

18.11 *02/05/1991*
Sepia ink on white paper,
14.5 x 20.4 cm
Collection of the artist

18.12 *03/06/1991*
Black ink on white paper,
14.5 x 20.4 cm
Collection of the artist

18.13 *03,04/06/1991*
Orange, blue and black ink and
graphite on white paper,
21.7 x 28 cm
Collection of the artist

WESTERN STAR

19.01 *28/02/1985*
Raw sienna and black ink on white
paper, 30.3 x 22.8 cm
Collection of the artist

19.02 *06/07/1985*
Raw sienna ink and graphite on
white paper, 30.4 x 22.8 cm
Collection of the artist

19.03 *10,11/07/1985*
Raw sienna ink and graphite on
white paper, 30.4 x 22.8 cm
Collection of the artist

19.04 *13/07/1985 (a)*
Raw sienna ink and graphite on
white paper, 30.4 x 22.7 cm
Collection of the artist

19.05 *13/07/1985 (b)*
Raw sienna, blue and black ink over
photocopy of photographs, on
white paper, with clear Mylar overlay, 21.6 cm x 27.9 cm
Collection of the artist

19.06 *15,22/07/1985*
Raw sienna and black ink and
acrylic on blue paper,
15.2 x 22.7 cm
Collection of the artist, courtesy of
the Drabinsky Gallery, Toronto

19.07 *24,27/07/1985*
Raw sienna and blue ink and
graphite on white paper,
30.4 x 22.8 cm
Collection of the artist

19.08 *28/07/1985*
Black ink on white paper,
22.7 x 15 cm
Collection of the artist

19.09 *29/07/1985*
Black ink on white paper,
22.5 x 15 cm
Collection of the artist

19.10 *29[?]/07/1985 and*
01,08/08/1985
Raw sienna, black and blue ink on
photocopy on white paper,
21.6 x 22.8 cm
Collection of the artist

19.11 *29[?]/07/1985 and 09/08/1985*
Raw sienna and blue ink on photocopy on white paper,
27.9 x 21.6 cm
Collection of the artist

19.12 *29[?],30/07/1985 and*
05/08/1985
Raw sienna ink, graphite and wash
on photocopy on white paper,
21.8 x 21.7 cm
Collection of the artist, courtesy of
the Drabinsky Gallery, Toronto

19.13 *09,12/08/1985*
Raw sienna and blue ink on photocopy on white paper,
24 x 21.5 cm
Collection of the artist

19.14 *18/09/1895*
Raw sienna ink and graphite on
white paper, 30.4 x 22.8 cm
Collection of the artist

TAXI

20.01 *10,11/01/1985*
Black ink and graphite on white
paper, 14.8 x 22.8 cm
Collection of the artist

20.02 *13/01/1985*
Black ink on white paper,
14.7 x 22.4 cm
Collection of the artist

20.03 *16/01/1985*
Black ink on white paper,
14.7 x 22.4 cm
Collection of the artist

20.04 *21/01/1985*
Black ink on white paper,
15 x 22.8 cm
Collection of the artist

20.05 *23/01/1985*
Black ink on white paper,
15 x 22.3 cm
Collection of the artist

20.06 *27/02/1985*
Raw sienna and black ink on paper,
30.3 x 22.8 cm
Collection of the artist

20.07 *28/02/1985*
Sepia ink and wash on white paper,
30.4 x 22.8 cm
Collection of the artist, courtesy of
the Drabinsky Gallery, Toronto

20.08 *04,05,11/03/1985*
Raw sienna and blue ink, graphite
and washes on card, 20.5 x 30.4 cm
Collection of the artist

20.09 *12,21,22,29/03/1985*
Raw sienna and blue ink, red acrylic
and graphite on card,
20.5 x 30.4 cm
Collection of the artist

20.10 *13/03/1985*
Raw sienna and black ink and
graphite on card, 20.5 x 30.4 cm
Collection of the artist

20.11 *21,28/03/1985*
Graphite over photocopy of photographs, on white paper,
27.8 x 21.6 cm
Collection of the artist

20.12 *04/04/1985*
Black ink on white paper,
27.8 x 21.5 cm
Collection of the artist

20.13 *05/04/1985*
Sepia ink and graphite on white
paper, 23 x 30.9 cm
Collection of the artist

TRAVELLER

21.01 *20/02/1992*
Black ink on white paper,
20.4 x 14.4 cm
Redpath Gallery, Vancouver

21.02 *06,17/02/1992*
Raw sienna, orange and blue ink on
grey paper, 28 x 21.7 cm
Redpath Gallery, Vancouver

21.03 *05,06/02/1992*
Black ink on white paper,
20.4 x 14.4 cm
Redpath Gallery, Vancouver

21.04 *17/07/1992*
Orange, blue and black ink on white
paper, 28 x 21.7 cm
Redpath Gallery, Vancouver

21.05 *20/02/1992*
Sepia and orange ink on grey-green
paper, 27.6 x 21.7 cm
Redpath Gallery, Vancouver

21.06 *22/02/1992*
Sepia ink on white paper,
20.4 x 14.4 cm
Redpath Gallery, Vancouver

21.07 *24/02/1992*
Black ink on white paper,
14.4 x 20.4 cm
Redpath Gallery, Vancouver

21.08 *24,26/02/1992*
Orange ink over photocopy of photocollage, on white paper,
21.6 x 32.3 cm
Redpath Gallery, Vancouver

21.09 *24/02/1992 ?*
Orange and blue ink on photocopy
on white paper, 28 x 21.6 cm
Redpath Gallery, Vancouver

21.10 *24/02/1992*
Orange, yellow and blue ink on
photocopy on white paper,
28 x 21.6 cm
Redpath Gallery, Vancouver

21.11 *24,25/02/1992 and 11/03/1992*
Orange, blue and black ink on white
paper, 21 x 21.6 cm
Redpath Gallery, Vancouver